OTHELLO

RETOLD IN PLAIN AND SIMPLE ENGLISH

SIDE BY SIDE VERSION

WILLIAM SHAKESPEARE

BookCap Study Guides
ANAHEIM, CALIFORNIA

Table of Contents

About This Series

The "Plain and Simple English" series started as a way of telling classics for the modern reader—being careful to preserve the themes and integrity of the original. Whether you want to understand Shakespeare a little more or are trying to get a better grasps of the Greek classics, there is a book waiting for you!

The series is expanding every month. Visit BookCaps.com to see all the books in the series, and while you are there join the Facebook page, so you are first to know when a new book comes out.

Characters

DUKE OF VENICE

    BRABANTIO, a Senator.

Other Senators.

GRATIANO, Brother to Brabantio

    LODOVICO, Kinsman to Brabantio

OTHELLO, a noble Moor, in the service of Venice

    CASSIO, his Lieutenant

IAGO, his Ancient

RODERIGO, a Venetian Gentleman

MONTANO, Othello's predecessor in the government of Cyprus

CLOWN, Servant to Othello

Herald

DESDEMONA, Daughter to Brabantio, and Wife to Othello

EMILIA, Wife to Iago

BIANCA, Mistress to Cassio

Officers, Gentlemen, Messenger, Musicians, Herald, Sailor,   Attendants, &c.

Play

Act I

Scene I. Venice. A street.

Enter RODERIGO and IAGO

RODERIGO

Tush! never tell me; I take it much unkindly | *Be quiet! Don't tell me this – I am already annoyed*
That thou, Iago, who hast had my purse | *That you, Iago, who already uses my money*
As if the strings were thine, shouldst know of this. | *As if it were yours, knows about this.*

IAGO

'Sblood, but you will not hear me: | *My god, you won't listen to me.*
If ever I did dream of such a matter, Abhor me. | *If I even so much as dreamed this were true, which I didn't, then go ahead and hate me.*

RODERIGO

Thou told'st me thou didst hold him in thy hate. | *You told me that you hated him.*

IAGO

Despise me, if I do not. Three great ones of the city, | *You can hate me if I was lying: I do hate him Three of the city's noblemen*

In personal suit to make me his lieutenant, | *Approached him personally and asked him to make me his next-in-command,*

Off-capp'd to him: and, by the faith of man, | *Even took their hats off to him. Moreover, I promise you,*

I know my price, I am worth no worse a place: | *I know my own value and that I deserve that position.*
But he; as loving his own pride and purposes, | *But he, because he is prideful and loves his own reasons most,*

Evades them, with a bombast circumstance | *Avoided their request with puffed up speech*
Horribly stuff'd with epithets of war; | *Full of military jargon and patriotic quotes,*
And, in conclusion, | *And, finally,*
Nonsuits my mediators; for, 'Certes,' says he, | *Rejected the noblemen, saying, "In fact,*
'I have already chose my officer.' | *I have already chosen my lieutenant."*
And what was he? | *Who did he choose?*
Forsooth, a great arithmetician, | *None other than the great statistician*
One Michael Cassio, a Florentine, | *Michael Cassio, from Florence,*
A fellow almost damn'd in a fair wife; | *A man almost cursed with such a beautiful wife,*
That never set a squadron in the field, | *A man who never moved troops in combat*
Nor the division of a battle knows | *And knows less of how an actual battle plays out*
More than a spinster; unless the bookish theoric, | *Than an unmarried woman – unless you count theories he read in books*

Wherein the toged consuls can propose | *That any gown-wearing politician can explain*
As masterly as he: mere prattle, without practise, | *As well as he can. He speaks simply to speak, and has no actual fighting*

Is all his soldiership. But he, sir, had the election: | *To back up his military life. But it is he, Roderigo, who was chosen:*

And I, of whom his eyes had seen the proof | *And as for me, whose bravery and talent he saw*
At Rhodes, at Cyprus and on other grounds | *At Rhodes and Cyprus and all over,*
Christian and heathen, must be be-lee'd and calm'd | *On Christian ground and foreign land, I must act calm*

By debitor and creditor: this counter-caster,

He, in good time, must his lieutenant be,
And I--God bless the mark!--his Moorship's ancient.

RODERIGO
By heaven, I rather would have been his hangman.

IAGO
Why, there's no remedy; 'tis the curse of service,

Preferment goes by letter and affection,
And not by old gradation, where each second
Stood heir to the first. Now, sir, be judge yourself,

Whether I in any just term am affined
To love the Moor.

RODERIGO
I would not follow him then.

IAGO
O, sir, content you;
I follow him to serve my turn upon him:

We cannot all be masters, nor all masters

Cannot be truly follow'd. You shall mark
Many a duteous and knee-crooking knave,
That, doting on his own obsequious bondage,

Wears out his time, much like his master's ass,

For nought but provender, and when he's old, cashier'd:

Whip me such honest knaves. Others there are

Who, trimm'd in forms and visages of duty,

Keep yet their hearts attending on themselves,
And, throwing but shows of service on their lords,

Do well thrive by them and when they have lined their coats
Do themselves homage: these fellows have some soul;

And such a one do I profess myself. For, sir,
It is as sure as you are Roderigo,
Were I the Moor, I would not be Iago:

In following him, I follow but myself;

In front of this accountant. So Cassio, this numbers-man,
Will become his lieutenant,
While I – how stupid – must hold the flag for the Moor general.

I swear, I would rather be his executioner.

And there is no cure for it all. It's the curse of the military life:
Promotions come from how liked one is,
And not from simple hierarchy where one Moves up to the next rank. Now, Roderigo, you tell me
If I am in any position
To love and respect the Moor general.

If it were me, I would not serve him.

Now don't be hasty:
I serve under him now, but for my own purposes –
After all, we cannot all be leaders, and leaders
Cannot all be followed. Take note
Of the servant who bows and does his duty,
Who fully attend to their obedience, their slavery,
And in the end is worn out like his master's donkey,
Both working for nothing but their food, and then terminated when too old.
We should punish such obedient servants. But there are others
Who know how to give the appearance of obedience
While focusing on themselves.
They give a performance of doing their duty to their masters
And in reality prosper by quietly stealing

And thus working for themselves. Servants like this are gutsy and bold,
And I admit I am one like that. To be sure,
As sure as your name is Roderigo,
If I were in the Moor's position, I would not want to switch places with Iago.
By serving him, I am really serving myself –

Heaven is my judge, not I for love and duty,
But seeming so, for my peculiar end:

For when my outward action doth demonstrate
The native act and figure of my heart
In compliment extern, 'tis not long after
But I will wear my heart upon my sleeve
For daws to peck at: I am not what I am.

RODERIGO
What a full fortune does the thicklips owe
If he can carry't thus!

IAGO
Call up her father,
Rouse him: make after him, poison his delight,
Proclaim him in the streets; incense her kinsmen,

And, though he in a fertile climate dwell,

Plague him with flies: though that his joy be joy,
Yet throw such changes of vexation on't,
As it may lose some colour.

RODERIGO
Here is her father's house; I'll call aloud.

IAGO
Do, with like timorous accent and dire yell
As when, by night and negligence, the fire
Is spied in populous cities.

RODERIGO
What, ho, Brabantio! Signior Brabantio, ho!

IAGO
Awake! what, ho, Brabantio! thieves! thieves!
thieves!

Look to your house, your daughter and your
bags!
Thieves! thieves!
BRABANTIO appears above, at a window

BRABANTIO
What is the reason of this terrible summons?
What is the matter there?

RODERIGO
Signior, is all your family within?

God knows I do not serve him for love or duty,
But just make it look like that while serving my own
goals.
If I ever act in such a way
That shows my inner self
Then before long I would be in danger:
One who wears his heart on his sleeve
Leaves it open for birds to peck at it. I am not who I
appear to be.

That thick-lipped Moor is lucky
If he can go through with this!

Speaking of which, call after her father
And wake him. Annoy him, spoil his happiness,
Shout at him in the streets, anger his and his
daughter's family
Until it seems like, though he lives in a temperate
climate,
He is plagued with flies. Though his joy may be real,
If it changes because of the confusions we put on it,
It may lose some of its brightness.

Here is her father's house; I'll call for him.

Do it as if you are frightened and yell
As if a fire started from negligence at night
Has been spotted in a city full of people.

Brabantio! Mister Brabantio, hey!

Wake up, Brabantio! Thieves are in your house!

Look around you and protect your daughter and your
possessions!
Thieves! Thieves!

Why are you shouting all of this?
What is the matter?

Sir, if your family at home?

IAGO
Are your doors lock'd?

And have you locked your doors?

BRABANTIO
Why, wherefore ask you this?

Why? Tell me why you are asking.

IAGO
'Zounds, sir, you're robb'd; for shame, put on your gown;

For God's sake, sir, you have been robbed!
Put your nightgown on.

Your heart is burst, you have lost half your soul;

Your heart is broken and you have lost a part
of your soul

Even now, now, very now, an old black ram
Is topping your white ewe. Arise, arise;

For now, right now, a black ram
Is riding your white female sheep. Get up, get
up;

Awake the snorting citizens with the bell,
Or else the devil will make a grandsire of you:

Wake up the sleeping people with the bell
Or it will be too late and the devil will give
you grandchildren.

Arise, I say.

Get up, I say.

BRABANTIO
What, have you lost your wits?

Have you gone crazy?

RODERIGO
Most reverend signior, do you know my voice?

My respected sir, do you recognize my voice?

BRABANTIO
Not I what are you?

No, who are you?

RODERIGO
My name is Roderigo.

I am Roderigo.

BRABANTIO
The worser welcome:
I have charged thee not to haunt about my doors:
In honest plainness thou hast heard me say
My daughter is not for thee; and now, in madness,

Even worse:
I have asked you not to come near my house
And very honestly told you
That my daughter is not for you. Now, as if
you are crazy,

Being full of supper and distempering draughts,
Upon malicious bravery, dost thou come

After dinner and likely drunk
With the evil courage a drunkard has, you
come here

To start my quiet.

And disturb me.

RODERIGO
Sir, sir, sir,--

Sir, sir, sir–

BRABANTIO
But thou must needs be sure
My spirit and my place have in them power
To make this bitter to thee.

Let me be clear:
I have the desire and the connections that can
Make this turn out very poorly for you.

RODERIGO
Patience, good sir.

Please wait, good sir.

BRABANTIO
What tell'st thou me of robbing? this is Venice;

My house is not a grange.

Why are you telling me my house is being robbed?
This is Venice –
I do not live out in the country.

RODERIGO
Most grave Brabantio,
In simple and pure soul I come to you.

Respectable Brabantio,
I have come with pure intentions and a simple
message.

IAGO
'Zounds, sir, you are one of those that will not

serve God, if the devil bid you. Because we
come to
do you service and you think we are ruffians,
you'll
have your daughter covered with a Barbary horse;

you'll have your nephews neigh to you;
you'll have
coursers for cousins and gennets for germans.

For God's sake, sir, you are so stubborn that you will
not
turn to God if even the devil asks you to. We come

for your benefit and yet you think we a
troublemakers;
so instead of listening, an African horse will mount
your daughter.
Your nephews will neigh at you, you will have

racing horses for cousins, and all of your close
relatives will become horses.

BRABANTIO
What profane wretch art thou?

Who are you, you rude pervert?

IAGO
I am one, sir, that comes to tell you your
daughter
and the Moor are now making the beast with
two backs.

I am someone, sir, who has come to you to tell you
you that your daughter
and the Moor general are having sex, like animals.

BRABANTIO
Thou art a villain.

You are an evil person.

IAGO
You are--a senator.

And you are a senator and statesman.

BRABANTIO
This thou shalt answer; I know thee, Roderigo.

Since I know you, Roderigo, you must respond to this.

RODERIGO
Sir, I will answer any thing. But, I beseech you,

If't be your pleasure and most wise consent,

As partly I find it is, that your fair daughter,
At this odd-even and dull watch o' the night,
Transported, with no worse nor better guard

Sir, I will tell you anything. But, please,

If you are pleased and contented with this
arrangement,
As I think you might be, that your beautiful daughter
At this late hour of the night,
Has left with no regular guard

But with a knave of common hire, a gondolier,
To the gross clasps of a lascivious Moor--

If this be known to you and your allowance,
We then have done you bold and saucy wrongs;

But if you know not this, my manners tell me
We have your wrong rebuke. Do not believe

That, from the sense of all civility,
I thus would play and trifle with your reverence:
Your daughter, if you have not given her leave,

I say again, hath made a gross revolt;

Tying her duty, beauty, wit and fortunes

In an extravagant and wheeling stranger

Of here and every where. Straight satisfy yourself:
If she be in her chamber or your house,
Let loose on me the justice of the state
For thus deluding you.

BRABANTIO
Strike on the tinder, ho!
Give me a taper! call up all my people!
This accident is not unlike my dream:

Belief of it oppresses me already.
Light, I say! light!
Exit above

IAGO
Farewell; for I must leave you:
It seems not meet, nor wholesome to my place,
To be produced--as, if I stay, I shall--
Against the Moor: for, I do know, the state,

However this may gall him with some cheque,
Cannot with safety cast him, for he's embark'd

With such loud reason to the Cyprus wars,

Which even now stand in act, that, for their souls,

Another of his fathom they have none,
To lead their business: in which regard,
Though I do hate him as I do hell-pains.

Yet, for necessity of present life,

---

*But with just hired commoner, a boatman,
To the disgusting embrace of the lustful Moor—*

*If you already know this and are allowing it
Then we have done you a very great evil in coming here.*

*But if you do not know this, I think
You are wrongly accusing us. You should not think*

*That, opposite of any sort of politeness,
I would disturb you and mess with you.*

*Your daughter, if you have not allowed her to leave,
I will repeat, has disgustingly rebelled against you*

By giving her respect, beauty, intelligence, and wealth

To an extravagant and tricky man who is a stranger

*Here and everywhere. Now see for yourself:
If she is still in her room or in your house,
Then punish me as the state allows
For tricking you.*

*Someone light a match!
Give me a candle! Wake my servants!
What you have told me is similar to a dream I have had –*

*Believing it as possible already haunts me.
Give me a light, I say! A light!*

*Goodbye, I must go
Since it is not good, or right since I serve him,
To be seen – which I will if I stay here –
As against the Moor. Especially because I know that the senator,*

*However this may offend and upset him,
Cannot easily get rid of him, since the Moor is leaving*

With clear and understood reason to Cyprus for the wars.

Even now these wars are raging and the statesmen

*Do not have another general like him
To lead their war efforts. I admit this
Even though I hate him as I would the fires of hell.*

So it is necessary for now

I must show out a flag and sign of love,
Which is indeed but sign. That you shall
surely find him,
Lead to the Sagittary the raised search;
And there will I be with him. So, farewell.
Exit
Enter, below, BRABANTIO, and Servants with torches

That I carry his flag and act like I love him,
Which as I said is only an act.
So that you definitely find him tonight,
Take the search party to the Arsenal
And I will already be there with him. Goodbye.

BRABANTIO
It is too true an evil: gone she is;
And what's to come of my despised time
Is nought but bitterness. Now, Roderigo,
Where didst thou see her? O unhappy girl!
With the Moor, say'st thou?
Who would be a father!
How didst thou know 'twas she?
O she deceives me
Past thought! What said she to you?
Get more tapers:
Raise all my kindred. Are they married,
think you?

Is it true that she's gone.
The rest of my life will be nothing without her
Where did you see her, Roderigo? That like unhappy
brat.
Did you see her with the Moor
Who would want to be her father!
How did you know it was her?
Does she really think she can trick me so easily?
What did she say to you?
Get me more candles,
And wake up my relatives. Do you think they are
married?

RODERIGO
Truly, I think they are.

Truly, I think they are.

BRABANTIO
O heaven! How got she out?
O treason of the blood!
Fathers, from hence trust not your daughters'
minds
By what you see them act. Is there not charms
By which the property of youth and maidhood
May be abused? Have you not read, Roderigo,
Of some such thing?

How on Earth did she get out?
My own relatives conspire against me!
Fathers, never trust your daughters just because
act innocent and good!
They are under an evil spell.
Is there any spell that can't lead a young girl away?
Have you ever heard of something like that,
Roderigo?

RODERIGO
Yes, sir, I have indeed.

Yes, sir, I have indeed.

BRABANTIO
Call up my brother. O, would you had had her!
Some one way, some another. Do you know
Where we may apprehend her and the Moor?

Call for my brother. Oh, now I wish you married her!
Some go one way, some go another. Do you know
Where we will find her and the Moor?

RODERIGO
I think I can discover him, if you please,
To get good guard and go along with me.

I think I know where he is. Please,
Get a good party of your guards and come with me.

BRABANTIO
Pray you, lead on. At every house I'll call;
I may command at most. Get weapons, ho!

I beg you to lead us. I will call at every house –
I can at least command men to join. Hey, arm
yourselves!

I may command at most. Get weapons, ho!

And raise some special officers of night.
On, good Roderigo: I'll deserve your pains.

Exeunt

I can at least command men to join. Hey, arm yourselves!
And XXX
Go forward, good Roderigo. You will be rewarded for your hard work.

Scene II. Another street.

Enter OTHELLO, IAGO, and Attendants with torches

IAGO
Though in the trade of war I have slain men,
Yet do I hold it very stuff o' the conscience
To do no contrived murder: I lack iniquity
Sometimes to do me service: nine or ten times

I had thought to have yerk'd him here under the ribs.

OTHELLO
'Tis better as it is.

IAGO
Nay, but he prated,
And spoke such scurvy and provoking terms
Against your honour
That, with the little godliness I have,
I did full hard forbear him. But, I pray you, sir,
Are you fast married? Be assured of this,

That the magnifico is much beloved,
And hath in his effect a voice potential
As double as the duke's: he will divorce you;
Or put upon you what restraint and grievance
The law, with all his might to enforce it on,
Will give him cable.

OTHELLO
Let him do his spite:
My services which I have done the signiory
Shall out-tongue his complaints. 'Tis yet to know,--

Which, when I know that boasting is an honour,
I shall promulgate--I fetch my life and being
From men of royal siege, and my demerits
May speak unbonneted to as proud a fortune

As this that I have reach'd: for know, Iago,

But that I love the gentle Desdemona,
I would not my unhoused free condition

Put into circumscription and confine
For the sea's worth. But, look! what lights come yond?

Though I have killed men in war,
I think it is the makeup of a good character
To not commit murder. I lack the evil
That would sometimes help me. Nine or ten times
I thought to simply stab him through his ribs.

It is better that you didn't.

No, he swore
And said such nasty and offensive things
Against you
That, with all the patience I could muster,
I listened to him say. But, I must ask, sir,
Are you securely married? Because you should know
That Brabantio is very respected and loved –
He has a voice worth potentially
Twice the duke's. He will force you to divorce
Or will try to punish you according to
The law, with all his strength,
As much as the law allows.

He can do his worst:
All that I have done for the government
Will outweigh his complaints against me. This is not known about me –
If it is ever honorable to boast
Then I will let it known widely – but my life
Comes from a royal line, and my worth
Can show that I have as great a wealth and position
As the woman I've married. And know this, Iago:
Unless I loved Desdemona,
I would never have ruined my bachelorhood and freedom
By adding the fence of marriage –
Not for an ocean's amount of money. But wait, what are those lights?

IAGO
Those are the raised father and his friends:

You were best go in.

Those belong to the angry father and his friends.
You should go inside and out of sight.

OTHELLO
Not I, I must be found:
My parts, my title and my perfect soul

Shall manifest me rightly. Is it they?

No, I will let them come to me.
My qualities, my rank, and my lack of wrongdoing
Will prove me in the right. Is that them?

IAGO
By Janus, I think no.
Enter CASSIO, and certain Officers with torches

Actually no, I don't think so.

OTHELL
The servants of the duke, and my lieutenant.

The goodness of the night upon you, friends!
What is the news?

It is the duke's servants and my new lieutenant, Cassio.
I hope you are well, friends!
Why do you come?

CASSIO
The duke does greet you, general,

And he requires your haste-post-haste appearance,

Even on the instant.

The duke has sent us to greet you, general,
And he requests your presence right away,
Immediately.

OTHELLO
What is the matter, think you?

Do you know what the matter is?

CASSIO
Something from Cyprus as I may divine:
It is a business of some heat: the galleys

Have sent a dozen sequent messengers
This very night at one another's heels,
And many of the consuls, raised and met,

Are at the duke's already: you have been hotly call'd for;

When, being not at your lodging to be found,

The senate hath sent about three several guests
To search you out.

I think it is something about Cyprus,
And it seems to be important. The warships
Have sent a dozen messengers
Tonight, one after another,
And many of the statesmen have woken and are here
With the duke. You were quickly asked for
And when you were not at found at your home,
Three different groups were sent
To find you.

OTHELLO
'Tis well I am found by you.

I will but spend a word here in the house,

It's good you are the one who found me.
I have to spend a minute here in this house,

And go with you.
Exit

And then will go with you.

CASSIO
Ancient, what makes he here?

Officer, what business does he have here?

IAGO
'Faith, he to-night hath boarded a land carack:

If it prove lawful prize, he's made for ever.

Truly, tonight he has boarded a large ship full of treasure,
And as long as it is and remains legal, he will be a made man forever.

CASSIO
I do not understand.

What are you talking about?

IAGO
He's married.

He's married.

CASSIO
To who?
Re-enter OTHELLO

To who?

IAGO
Marry, to--Come, captain, will you go?

Why, to – My captain, shall we go?

OTHELLO
Have with you.

Yes, let's go.

CASSIO
Here comes another troop to seek for you.

Here comes another group looking for you.

IAGO
It is Brabantio. General, be advised;
He comes to bad intent.
Enter BRABANTIO, RODERIGO, and Officers with torches and weapons

It is Brabantio. Be careful, general,
Because he intends you harm.

OTHELLO
Holla! stand there!

Hello, stay there!

RODERIGO
Signior, it is the Moor.

Sir, it is the Moor.

BRABANTIO
Down with him, thief!
They draw on both sides

Get that thief!

IAGO
You, Roderigo! come, sir, I am for you.

Roderigo, come towards me, I'll fight you.

OTHELLO

Keep up your bright swords, for the dew will rust them.

Good signior, you shall more command with years

Than with your weapons.

Keep your swords in their sheaths so the dew does not rust them.
Good sir, the years you have served the government will make me respect you
More than fighting you will.

BRABANTIO

O thou foul thief, where hast thou stow'd my daughter?

Damn'd as thou art, thou hast enchanted her;

For I'll refer me to all things of sense,
If she in chains of magic were not bound,
Whether a maid so tender, fair and happy,
So opposite to marriage that she shunned

The wealthy curled darlings of our nation,
Would ever have, to incur a general mock,

Run from her guardage to the sooty bosom
Of such a thing as thou, to fear, not to delight.

Judge me the world, if 'tis not gross in sense

That thou hast practised on her with foul charms,
Abused her delicate youth with drugs or minerals

That weaken motion: I'll have't disputed on;

'Tis probable and palpable to thinking.
I therefore apprehend and do attach thee

For an abuser of the world, a practiser
Of arts inhibited and out of warrant.
Lay hold upon him: if he do resist,
Subdue him at his peril.

O you evil thief, where have you hidden my daughter?
Since you are a damned soul, I know you put a spell on her.
All good and common sense says that,
Unless she were enchanted through magic,
A woman so gentle, beautiful, and happy,
A woman who was against marriage so much that she turned away
The wealthy noblemen of our nation,
This woman would never do something others would see fit to make jokes at
Like run from her home to your black breast.
Someone like you should be feared, not enjoyed.
The whole world may judge me if it's not obvious
That you have practiced evil magic on her
And taken advantage of her naive youth through drugs
That make one unable to move. I would go to court over the matter;
It's what most likely happened.
Therefore, I will take you and see that you are tried
As a criminal, a practicer
Of dark magic.
Take him: if he resists arrest
Then forcefully hold him down.

OTHELLO

Hold your hands,
Both you of my inclining, and the rest:
Were it my cue to fight, I should have known it
Without a prompter. Where will you that I go

To answer this your charge?

Do not touch me,
Neither you on my side or the rest of you.
If it were necessary to fight, I would not
Need someone to tell me. Where do you want me to go
In order to respond to your accusations?

BRABANTIO

To prison, till fit time
Of law and course of direct session
Call thee to answer.

To prison until the time
That the law sees fit to take you to court
And ask you to testify.

OTHELLO
What if I do obey?
How may the duke be therewith satisfied,
Whose messengers are here about my side,
Upon some present business of the state
To bring me to him?
First Officer
'Tis true, most worthy signior;
The duke's in council and your noble self,
I am sure, is sent for.

BRABANTIO
How! the duke in council!
In this time of the night! Bring him away:
Mine's not an idle cause: the duke himself,
Or any of my brothers of the state,
Cannot but feel this wrong as 'twere their own;
For if such actions may have passage free,
Bond-slaves and pagans shall our statesmen be.

Exeunt

And if I obey,
Then how will the duke react,
Since he sent these messengers
On urgent, national business
To bring me to him?

It's true, worthy sir:
The duke has called a meeting and you, too,
I am sure, are asked to attend.

What? The duke has called a meeting!
This late at night! Take him away.
This is not some simple affair: the duke himself
And all of the other senators
Will feel how wrong this is, as if it happened to them.
If actions like this go unpunished,
Then slaves and pagans will become our rulers.

Scene III. A council-chamber.

The DUKE and Senators sitting at a table; Officers attending

DUKE OF VENICE
There is no composition in these news
That gives them credit.

Nothing about these messages
Makes me think that they are credible.

First Senator
Indeed, they are disproportion'd;
My letters say a hundred and seven galleys.

Yes, they give conflicting reports.
My letters say there are a hundred and seven
warships.

DUKE OF VENICE
And mine, a hundred and forty.

And mine says a hundred and forty.

Second Senator
And mine, two hundred:
But though they jump not on a just account,--
As in these cases, where the aim reports,

Mind says two hundred.
But though they give conflicting numbers –
Since it is often when one is reporting an
estimate

'Tis oft with difference--yet do they all confirm

For there to be different numbers – they all
report

A Turkish fleet, and bearing up to Cyprus.

That a Turkish fleet is moving to Cyprus.

DUKE OF VENICE
Nay, it is possible enough to judgment:
I do not so secure me in the error,
But the main article I do approve
In fearful sense.
Sailor

Right, that seems well confirmed.
I am not so taken by the inconsistency
That I miss the bigger issue, which
Frightens me.

[Within] What, ho! what, ho! what, ho!

Hello! Hello!

First Officer
A messenger from the galleys.
Enter a Sailor

Another messenger from the warships.

DUKE OF VENICE
Now, what's the business?

What have you come to tell us?

Sailor
The Turkish preparation makes for Rhodes;

The Turkish fleet is heading to Rhodes, not
Cyprus –

So was I bid report here to the state

This was what I was ordered to report to the
government

By Signior Angelo.

By Sir Angelo.

DUKE OF VENICE
How say you by this change?

What do you make of this change?

First Senator
This cannot be,
By no assay of reason: 'tis a pageant,
To keep us in false gaze. When we consider
The importancy of Cyprus to the Turk,
And let ourselves again but understand,
That as it more concerns the Turk than Rhodes,
So may he with more facile question bear it,

For that it stands not in such warlike brace,
But altogether lacks the abilities
That Rhodes is dress'd in: if we make thought of this,
We must not think the Turk is so unskillful

To leave that latest which concerns him first,

Neglecting an attempt of ease and gain,

To wake and wage a danger profitless.

DUKE OF VENICE
Nay, in all confidence, he's not for Rhodes.

First Officer
Here is more news.
Enter a Messenger

Messenger
The Ottomites, reverend and gracious,
Steering with due course towards the isle of Rhodes,
Have there injointed them with an after fleet.

First Senator
Ay, so I thought. How many, as you guess?

Messenger
Of thirty sail: and now they do restem
Their backward course, bearing with frank appearance
Their purposes toward Cyprus. Signior Montano,
Your trusty and most valiant servitor,
With his free duty recommends you thus,

And prays you to believe him.

DUKE OF VENICE
'Tis certain, then, for Cyprus.
Marcus Luccicos, is not he in town?

First Senator
He's now in Florence.

This cannot be true
By any argument. It's a show
To distract us. We must remember
The importance of Cyprus to the Turks.
This will force us to recognize
That it is more important than Rhodes –
Especially because the Turks can more easily take it
Since it is not equipped with defenses
And lacks the preparations and forces
That Rhodes has. These things considered,
We must not think that the Turks are so incompetent
That they would put off what they should do first,
That they would not take a place so easily taken as Cyprus
And instead would attack a dangerous place like Rhodes.

I agree, the Turks are certainly not heading to Rhodes.

Another messenger is coming.

The Turks, my revered and gracious leader,
Went to the island of Rhodes
Where they have joined with another fleet.

I thought so. How many ships, do you think?

Thirty ships, and now they are turning around
To their original course and clearly seem to
Be heading to Cyprus. Sir Montano,
Your trustworthy and brave servant,
Sent me to give you this report and asks for reinforcements,
And asks you to believe him.

That settles it: the Turks are going to Cyprus.
Is Marcus Luccicos here in town?

No, he's in Florence.

DUKE OF VENICE
Write from us to him; post-post-haste dispatch.

Write to him and send it immediately, as fast as possible.

First Senator
Here comes Brabantio and the valiant Moor.

Here comes Brabantio and Othello, the courageous Moor.

Enter BRABANTIO, OTHELLO, IAGO, RODERIGO, and Officers

DUKE OF VENICE
Valiant Othello, we must straight employ you
Against the general enemy Ottoman.
To BRABANTIO
I did not see you; welcome, gentle signior;
We lack'd your counsel and your help tonight.

*Brave Othello, we must order you to go
Against the Turkish enemy.*

*I did not see you there – welcome, good sir.
We have lacked your insight and help tonight.*

BRABANTIO
So did I yours. Good your grace, pardon me;

Neither my place nor aught I heard of business
Hath raised me from my bed, nor doth the general care

Take hold on me, for my particular grief
Is of so flood-gate and o'erbearing nature
That it engluts and swallows other sorrows

And it is still itself.

*And I lacked yours. Please, your grace, forgive me:
It was not from hearing of this war business
That made me get out of bed, nor was it general worry over the city
That woke me. My personal grief
Is so overbearing, like a flood,
That it overtakes and swallows all other sorrows and concerns
Without being satisfied.*

DUKE OF VENICE
Why, what's the matter?

What has happened?

BRABANTIO
My daughter! O, my daughter!

My daughter! O, my daughter!

ALL
Dead?

Dead?

BRABANTIO
Ay, to me;
She is abused, stol'n from me, and corrupted

By spells and medicines bought of mountebanks;

For nature so preposterously to err,

Being not deficient, blind, or lame of sense,

Sans witchcraft could not.

*Yes, she is dead to me at least.
She has been abused, stolen from me, and corrupted
By black magic and drugs given to her by deceivers.
Nature itself could not have made such a preposterous mistake,
Since she is not mentally ill, or blind, or paralyzed,
So it must be the fault of witchcraft.*

DUKE OF VENICE
Whoe'er he be that in this foul proceeding
Hath thus beguiled your daughter of herself
And you of her, the bloody book of law

You shall yourself read in the bitter letter
After your own sense, yea, though our proper son
Stood in your action.

Whoever the criminal is
Who has tricked your daughter
And taken her from you, you will use the full,
deadly laws
To prosecute him in its harsh solutions
As you see fit – even if it were my own son
Who did what you have said.

BRABANTIO
Humbly I thank your grace.
Here is the man, this Moor, whom now, it seems,
Your special mandate for the state-affairs
Hath hither brought.

I humbly thank you, your grace.
Here is the criminal: this Moor, who, it seems,
Your national interest problems
Have brought here.

ALL
We are very sorry for't.

We are sorry to hear this.

DUKE OF VENICE
[To OTHELLO] What, in your own part, can you
say to this?

How do you respond to this, Othello?

BRABANTIO
Nothing, but this is so.

He can say nothing, it is true.

OTHELLO
Most potent, grave, and reverend signiors,
My very noble and approved good masters,
That I have ta'en away this old man's daughter,

It is most true; true, I have married her:
The very head and front of my offending
Hath this extent, no more. Rude am I in my speech,

And little bless'd with the soft phrase of peace:

For since these arms of mine had seven years' pith,

Till now some nine moons wasted, they have used
Their dearest action in the tented field,
And little of this great world can I speak,
More than pertains to feats of broil and battle,
And therefore little shall I grace my cause
In speaking for myself. Yet, by your gracious patience,

I will a round unvarnish'd tale deliver
Of my whole course of love; what drugs, what charms,

What conjuration and what mighty magic,
For such proceeding I am charged withal,
I won his daughter.

Powerful, serious, and revered sirs,
My noble and good masters,
That I have taken this old man's daughter
from him
Is true: I have married her.
The offenses Brabantio mentioned
Are true only in this. I am not a skilled
speaker
And do not know how to talk peacefully and
smoothly:
Since I was seven years old, and these arms
had seven years of muscle,
Until nine months ago, I have used these arms
For action in the battlefield.
I can't say much about this great world
Unless it is about war and battle,
And therefore I will only say a little
In speaking for my defense. But, by your
patience, gracious Duke,
I will tell you straightforwardly the story
Of how we fell in love – including the drugs,
magic charms,
Spells, and darks arts,
Since that is what I am charged of using,
I used to win his daughter.

BRABANTIO
A maiden never bold;
Of spirit so still and quiet, that her motion
Blush'd at herself; and she, in spite of nature,

Of years, of country, credit, every thing,

To fall in love with what she fear'd to look on!

It is a judgment maim'd and most imperfect
That will confess perfection so could err

Against all rules of nature, and must be driven

To find out practises of cunning hell,

Why this should be. I therefore vouch again

That with some mixtures powerful o'er the blood,

Or with some dram conjured to this effect,
He wrought upon her.

DUKE OF VENICE
To vouch this, is no proof,
Without more wider and more overt test
Than these thin habits and poor likelihoods

Of modern seeming do prefer against him.

First Senator
But, Othello, speak:
Did you by indirect and forced courses

Subdue and poison this young maid's affections?

Or came it by request and such fair question

As soul to soul affordeth?

OTHELLO
I do beseech you,
Send for the lady to the Sagittary,
And let her speak of me before her father:

If you do find me foul in her report,
The trust, the office I do hold of you,
Not only take away, but let your sentence
Even fall upon my life.

She was never bold,
But always calm and quiet, so pure that
She would blush at herself. And you are
saying that she, against nature,
Against difference in age, and country, and
upbringing, against everything,
Would fall in love with who she was afraid to
look at!
Only a poor and imperfect judgment
Could argue that a perfect person could do
something so wrong
Against all rules of nature – one must be
forced
To think that it is hell itself and the tricks of
the devil
That would make this happen. Therefore, I
again hold
That some sort of powerful drug to change her
desires
Or magical spell
Has been given to her by him.

To hold to this is not proof –
One needs clear evidence, more
Than the customs and poor accusations of
going against
What you think is acceptable must stand
against him.

But tell us, Othello:
Did you use any underhanded or manipulative
means
To persuade and poison this young girl's
desires?
Or did your marriage come from a simple
request and a fair question,
Making it an equal decision?

I beg you
To bring the lady herself here to the Armory
So that she can speak plainly of me in front of
her father.
If in her report you find me evil,
Then the position and rank you have given me
Should be taken away, and your sentence
Should also cost me my life.

DUKE OF VENICE
Fetch Desdemona hither.

Bring Desdemona here.

OTHELLO
Ancient, conduct them: you best know the place.
Exeunt IAGO and Attendants
And, till she come, as truly as to heaven
I do confess the vices of my blood,
So justly to your grave ears I'll present
How I did thrive in this fair lady's love,
And she in mine.

Iago, lead them – you know where she is.

While we wait, as honestly
As I confess my sins to God,
I will record to your serious listening
How I grew in this beautiful lady's love,
And how she grew in mine.

DUKE OF VENICE
Say it, Othello.

Tell us, Othello.

OTHELLO
Her father loved me; oft invited me;

Her father has loved me and often invited me
to their home

Still question'd me the story of my life,

Where he asked me to recount the story of my
life,

From year to year, the battles, sieges, fortunes,
That I have passed.
I ran it through, even from my boyish days,
To the very moment that he bade me tell it;

Each year, the battles and sieges and fortunes,
That I have experienced.
I told it all, even stories from my childhood,
Everything up to the moment I was talking to
him.

Wherein I spake of most disastrous chances,
Of moving accidents by flood and field
Of hair-breadth scapes i' the imminent deadly breach,
Of being taken by the insolent foe
And sold to slavery, of my redemption thence
And portance in my travels' history:
Wherein of antres vast and deserts idle,
Rough quarries, rocks and hills whose heads touch
Heaven
It was my hint to speak,--such was the process;

I spoke of dangerous risks,
Of adventures on sea and land,
Of escaping by a hair from imminent death,
Of being taken by an enemy
And sold into slavery, of buying my freedom.
I told him also of the travels I have had,
Of deep caves and empty deserts,
Rocky places, mountains and hills that reach
up to heaven,
I spoke about everything – that was the
routine –

And of the Cannibals that each other eat,
The Anthropophagi and men whose heads

About Cannibals that eat each other
Called the Anthropophagi and those whose
heads

Do grow beneath their shoulders. This to hear
Would Desdemona seriously incline:
But still the house-affairs would draw her thence:

Grow beneath their shoulders. All the while
Desdemona would lean in and listen seriously,
Though soon enough she would have to leave
to do chores,

Which ever as she could with haste dispatch,
She'ld come again, and with a greedy ear
Devour up my discourse: which I observing,
Took once a pliant hour, and found good means
To draw from her a prayer of earnest heart
That I would all my pilgrimage dilate,
Whereof by parcels she had something heard,
But not intentively: I did consent,

Which she did quickly so she could return
And listen again, wanting to hear
Everything I was saying. I observed all of this
And when I was relaxing, I was able
To speak with her. She prayed earnestly
That I would tell her of everything
Since she had heard some parts of the stories
But not everything. I agreed,

And often did beguile her of her tears,
When I did speak of some distressful stroke
That my youth suffer'd. My story being done,

She gave me for my pains a world of sighs:
She swore, in faith, twas strange, 'twas passing strange,
'Twas pitiful, 'twas wondrous pitiful:
She wish'd she had not heard it, yet she wish'd

That heaven had made her such a man: she thank'd me,

And bade me, if I had a friend that loved her,

I should but teach him how to tell my story.
And that would woo her. Upon this hint I spake:

She loved me for the dangers I had pass'd,

And I loved her that she did pity them.

This only is the witchcraft I have used:
Here comes the lady; let her witness it.

Enter DESDEMONA, IAGO, and Attendants

DUKE OF VENICE
I think this tale would win my daughter too.

Good Brabantio,
Take up this mangled matter at the best:
Men do their broken weapons rather use

Than their bare hands.

BRABANTIO
I pray you, hear her speak:
If she confess that she was half the wooer,
Destruction on my head, if my bad blame

Light on the man! Come hither, gentle mistress:

Do you perceive in all this noble company
Where most you owe obedience?

DESDEMONA
My noble father,
I do perceive here a divided duty:
To you I am bound for life and education;
My life and education both do learn me
How to respect you; you are the lord of duty;

And often my stories caused her to cry
When I spoke of some hardship
That I had suffered when I was younger. When I had finished,
She sighed at the thought of my former pains
And told me how strange
And sad, truly sad, my story was.
She said she wished that she had not heard it and yet that she wished
That heaven had made a man like me for her. She thanked me
And requested that, if I ever had a friend who loved her,
I would teach him how to tell a story like me,
And that she would fall in love with such a man. I took this hint and spoke to her.
She loved me for the dangerous events I had experienced
And I loved her because she felt so strongly for me from the stories.
This is the only magic that I used.
Here comes Desdemona herself, she can support what I have said.

I think such a story would win my daughter's heart, as well.
Brabantio,
Try to make the most of this business.
Using a broken weapon, even if its not what you want, is better
Than using your empty, bare hands.

Please, here her side.
If she agrees and says it was mutual,
Then I curse myself for allowing mistaken blame
To come to someone. Come here, gentle woman:
Do you understand in this group of noblemen
To which one you owe your strongest obedience?

My noble father,
I am conflicted:
I owe my life and education to you
And both have taught me
To respect you. You are the lord I give my duty to,

I am hitherto your daughter: but here's my husband,

And so much duty as my mother show'd
To you, preferring you before her father,
So much I challenge that I may profess
Due to the Moor my lord.

BRABANTIO
God be wi' you! I have done.
Please it your grace, on to the state-affairs:

I had rather to adopt a child than get it.
Come hither, Moor:
I here do give thee that with all my heart
Which, but thou hast already, with all my heart

I would keep from thee. For your sake, jewel,

I am glad at soul I have no other child:

For thy escape would teach me tyranny,

To hang clogs on them. I have done, my lord.

DUKE OF VENICE
Let me speak like yourself, and lay a sentence,

Which, as a grise or step, may help these lovers.
When remedies are past, the griefs are ended

By seeing the worst, which late on hopes depended.

To mourn a mischief that is past and gone
Is the next way to draw new mischief on.
What cannot be preserved when fortune takes
Patience her injury a mockery makes.

The robb'd that smiles steals something from the thief;

He robs himself that spends a bootless grief.

BRABANTIO
So let the Turk of Cyprus us beguile;
We lose it not, so long as we can smile.
He bears the sentence well that nothing bears

But the free comfort which from thence he hears,

But he bears both the sentence and the sorrow

And up to this point I am your daughter. But over here is my husband,
And as my mother gave more obedience
You over her own father,
So too I wish to announce
My obedience to the Moor.

God be with you! I am done with this.
Please, your grace, move on to the national business:
I would rather adopt a child.
Come here, Moor:
I hereby give you with all my heart
That which if you didn't already have it, with all my heart
I would keep from you. For your sake, daughter,
I am glad in my soul that I have no other child,
For your running off would make me become tyrannous,
And want to tie them up at home. I am done, my lord.

Let me say something briefly, and give you some advice
Which may help you forgive these lovers.
When it is too late to fix something, a sad situation often ends
By seeing it in the worst light since our hopes rested on fixing it.
To stay sad when that situation is over
Is the sure way to bring on new troubles.
Luck may take something we want to keep,
But being patient through that situation mocks and injures Luck.
He who smiles while he is being robbed steals something from the thief,
But he who grieves robs himself of even more

Then we should let the Turks take Cyprus:
As long as we smile, we do not really lose it.
-It's easy to give advice when you do not have to feel the pain
And instead can sit in your comfort and hear of others' pain.
But he who has to bear the pain and listen to such advice

That, to pay grief, must of poor patience borrow.

These sentences, to sugar, or to gall,
Being strong on both sides, are equivocal:

But words are words; I never yet did hear

That the bruised heart was pierced through the ear.

I humbly beseech you, proceed to the affairs of state.

DUKE OF VENICE
The Turk with a most mighty preparation makes for
Cyprus. Othello, the fortitude of the place is best
known to you; and though we have there a substitute

of most allowed sufficiency, yet opinion, a
sovereign mistress of effects, throws a more safer

voice on you: you must therefore be content to
slubber the gloss of your new fortunes with this

more stubborn and boisterous expedition.

OTHELLO
The tyrant custom, most grave senators,
Hath made the flinty and steel couch of war
My thrice-driven bed of down: I do agnise

A natural and prompt alacrity
I find in hardness, and do undertake
These present wars against the Ottomites.
Most humbly therefore bending to your state,

I crave fit disposition for my wife.

Due reference of place and exhibition,
With such accommodation and besort
As levels with her breeding.

DUKE OF VENICE
If you please,
Be't at her father's.

BRABANTIO
I'll not have it so.

OTHELLO
Nor I.

---

*Might lose his patience from the weight of it
all.
Your advice, both sweet and sour,
Is so extremely sweet and sour that it ends up
meaning nothing.
But words are only words and I have never
heard
Of someone's pain being comforted by
hearing talk.
Please, move on to the state affairs.*

*The Turk with a great fleet is heading to
Cyprus. Othello, the strength of Cyprus is best
known to you and though we have an officer
there
who is very good, the opinion here,
which ultimately makes decisions, is that you
are a better
option. Therefore, you must be ok
with putting off the celebrations of your
marriage
for this expedition.*

*The military life, respected senators,
Has made the dangerous bed of war
As comfortable as a bed of down feathers. I
have
A natural readiness
That has come from hardness and will take on
These battles against the Turks.
I humbly obey, but also ask the state for a
favor
Since I desire the right environment for my
wife.
Please provide her with a place to to live
As well as the accommodations and people
That match her high place in society.*

*If you don't mind,
She can stay at her father's.*

I will not allow it.

I won't either.

DESDEMONA
Nor I; I would not there reside,
To put my father in impatient thoughts
By being in his eye. Most gracious duke,
To my unfolding lend your prosperous ear;
And let me find a charter in your voice,
To assist my simpleness.

Neither will I. I would not want to stay there
And tempt my father to become upset
By being seen by him. Gracious duke,
Please listen to my request
And let me hear you help me
By allowing a simple favor.

DUKE OF VENICE
What would You, Desdemona?

What would you like, Desdemona?

DESDEMONA
That I did love the Moor to live with him,

My downright violence and storm of fortunes
May trumpet to the world: my heart's subdued
Even to the very quality of my lord:

I saw Othello's visage in his mind,
And to his honour and his valiant parts
Did I my soul and fortunes consecrate.

So that, dear lords, if I be left behind,
A moth of peace, and he go to the war,
The rites for which I love him are bereft me,

And I a heavy interim shall support
By his dear absence. Let me go with him.

When I decided to love the Moor, I decided to
live with him,
As the violence and poor fortunes I now have
Attest to everyone. My heart has become
Similar to Othello's – I am part soldier now,
too.
I saw Othello truly when I saw his mind,
And he has such honor and courage
That I pledged my soul and life to respect
these things.
So, noblemen, if I am left here
In peace, and he goes off to war,
Then everything I pledged to him are taken
away from me,
And I must bear a heavy weight
While he is gone. Let me go with him.

OTHELLO
Let her have your voices.
Vouch with me, heaven, I therefore beg it not,
To please the palate of my appetite,
Nor to comply with heat--the young affects

In me defunct--and proper satisfaction.
But to be free and bounteous to her mind:
And heaven defend your good souls, that you think
I will your serious and great business scant

For she is with me: no, when light-wing'd toys

Of feather'd Cupid seal with wanton dullness
My speculative and officed instruments,
That my disports corrupt and taint my business,

Let housewives make a skillet of my helm,

And all indign and base adversities
Make head against my estimation!

Please let her do this.
Let me be clear: I do not ask you to do this
To satisfy my sexual needs
Or lusting desires since these young
characteristics
Are no longer in me.
But I love her for her brilliant mind.
And, you are wrong if you think
That I will neglect the serious work you sent
me to do
Because she is with me – this won't happen. If
heady love
From Cupid ever dulls
My capabilities as a general,
Or makes me obsessed with pleasure, or ruins
my work,
Then retire me and let housewives use my
helmet as a frying pan.
Every unworthy and awful trait
Should thus be accounted against my
reputation!

DUKE OF VENICE
Be it as you shall privately determine,
Either for her stay or going: the affair cries haste,

And speed must answer it.

Answer it yourselves in private,
But whether she stays or goes, the war won't wait
So decide quickly.

First Senator
You must away to-night.

Othello must leave tonight.

OTHELLO
With all my heart.

I will, certainly.

DUKE OF VENICE
At nine i' the morning here we'll meet again.

Othello, leave some officer behind,
And he shall our commission bring to you;
With such things else of quality and respect
As doth import you.

We will meet here tomorrow at nine in the morning.
Othello, leave an officer behind
To bring your commission to you
Alongside anythings else you need
That you find important.

OTHELLO
So please your grace, my ancient;

A man he is of honest and trust:
To his conveyance I assign my wife,

With what else needful your good grace shall think
To be sent after me.

If you agree to it, let me leave my flagbearer and ensign, Iago.
He is an honest and trustworthy man
So I will leave him responsible for bringing my wife
Along with whatever else you think I need
To be sent along after I leave.

DUKE OF VENICE
Let it be so.
Good night to every one.
To BRABANTIO
And, noble signior,
If virtue no delighted beauty lack,
Your son-in-law is far more fair than black.

We will do that.
Goodnight, everyone.

And, noble sir,
If good character was beautiful in itself,
Then your new son-in-law is much more beautiful than his skin color.

First Senator
Adieu, brave Moor, use Desdemona well.

Goodbye, brave Othello. Take care of Desdemona.

BRABANTIO
Look to her, Moor, if thou hast eyes to see:
She has deceived her father, and may thee.

Be watchful, Moor, and be careful:
She tricked me: who says she won't trick you as well?

Exeunt DUKE OF VENICE, Senators, Officers, & c

OTHELLO
My life upon her faith! Honest Iago,

My Desdemona must I leave to thee:
I prithee, let thy wife attend on her:

I will stake my life on her faithfulness! Honest Iago,
I must leave Desdemona to you.
Please, let your wife wait on her

And bring them after in the best advantage.
Come, Desdemona: I have but an hour
Of love, of worldly matters and direction,
To spend with thee: we must obey the time.
Exeunt OTHELLO and DESDEMONA

RODERIGO
Iago,--

IAGO
What say'st thou, noble heart?

RODERIGO
What will I do, thinkest thou?

IAGO
Why, go to bed, and sleep.

RODERIGO
I will incontinently drown myself.

IAGO
If thou dost, I shall never love thee after. Why,

thou silly gentleman!

RODERIGO
It is silliness to live when to live is torment; and

then have we a prescription to die when death is our
physician.

IAGO
O villainous! I have looked upon the world for four
times seven years; and since I could distinguish
betwixt a benefit and an injury, I never found man

that knew how to love himself. Ere I would say, I

would drown myself for the love of a guinea-hen, I

would change my humanity with a baboon.

RODERIGO
What should I do? I confess it is my shame to be so

fond; but it is not in my virtue to amend it.

IAGO
Virtue! a fig! 'tis in ourselves that we are thus

And bring them both when you can.
Come, Desdemona, I only have an hour,
before attending to my duties,
To spend loving you. We must be quick.

Iago–

Yes, good man?

What do you think I should do?

You should go to bed and sleep.

Perhaps I will drown myself.

If you do, I will never think well of you
afterwards.
You are absurd!

No, it is absurd to live life when it is so
painful,
especially when we have a prescription to end
the pain through death.

What an evil thought! I have lived for
28 years, and not once,
whether a man was lucky or unlucky, did I
ever find
someone who could love himself. Before I
would ever say something
like "I would drown myself because of loving
this woman whom I can't have,"
I would give up my humanity and become a
monkey instead.

So what should I do? I know it is shameful to
be so
obsessed, but it's not in my personality to fix
it.

Personality is meaningless! We have the
power to become this person

or thus. Our bodies are our gardens, to the which
our wills are gardeners: so that if we will plant
nettles, or sow lettuce, set hyssop and weed up
thyme, supply it with one gender of herbs, or
distract it with many, either to have it sterile

with idleness, or manured with industry, why, the

power and corrigible authority of this lies in our

wills. If the balance of our lives had not one
scale of reason to poise another of sensuality, the
blood and baseness of our natures would conduct us
to most preposterous conclusions: but we have

reason to cool our raging motions, our carnal
stings, our unbitted lusts, whereof I take this that
you call love to be a sect or scion.

RODERIGO
It cannot be.

IAGO
It is merely a lust of the blood and a permission of
the will. Come, be a man. Drown thyself! Drown

cats and blind puppies. I have professed me thy
friend and I confess me knit to thy deserving with
cables of perdurable toughness; I could never
better stead thee than now. Put money in thy

purse; follow thou the wars; defeat thy favour with

an usurped beard; I say, put money in thy purse. It
cannot be that Desdemona should long continue her
love to the Moor,-- put money in thy purse,--nor he

his to her: it was a violent commencement, and thou

shalt see an answerable sequestration:--put but
money in thy purse. These Moors are changeable in
their wills: fill thy purse with money:--the food
that to him now is as luscious as locusts, shall be
to him shortly as bitter as coloquintida. She must
change for youth: when she is sated with his body,

she will find the error of her choice: she must

have change, she must: therefore put money in thy

purse. If thou wilt needs damn thyself, do it a

---

or that person. Who we are is like a garden,
and our wills are the gardeners. If we plant
thorns, or lettuce, or hyssop, or
thyme, plant only one kind of plant or
plant many different ones, if the garden
produces nothing
because we haven't done anything to it, or if it
has been worked and manured, well
the power and authority for how it turns out is
in our
wills. If our psychologies did not include
reason to fight against our emotional desires,
then everything we feel would lead us
to absurd decisions based only on emotion.
But, we have
reason to temper our desires and fleshly
impulses and lusts – and I think that what
you call love is just another kind of impulse.

That's not true.

It's only a strong desire that you have allowed
by your will. Come on, be a man. Drown
yourself, how absurd! You drown
cats and blind puppies. I have said before that
I am your friend, and I will stay close to you
with unbreakable bonds: but never before
have I been a better friend than now. Make
money,
watch how the wars turn out, and fight against
your feelings
like a man – and make money.
Desdemona will not continue to be
in love with the Moor for long – make more
money – nor
will he keep loving her. It happened quickly
and you
will see them come apart quickly as well – so
make money. Moors change their minds
on a whim – make more money – and what he
thinks now is sweet and filling will soon
become as bitter as a crabapple. She will
prefer a younger man when she is tired on his
body,
and will think she made a wrong decision. She
must
have someone different, so keep making
money.
If you want to go to hell, do it

more delicate way than drowning. Make all the money

thou canst: if sanctimony and a frail vow betwixt

an erring barbarian and a supersubtle Venetian not
too hard for my wits and all the tribe of hell, thou

shalt enjoy her; therefore make money. A pox of

drowning thyself! it is clean out of the way: seek
thou rather to be hanged in compassing thy joy than

to be drowned and go without her.

RODERIGO
Wilt thou be fast to my hopes, if I depend on
the issue?

IAGO
Thou art sure of me:--go, make money:--I have told
thee often, and I re-tell thee again and again, I
hate the Moor: my cause is hearted; thine hath no

less reason. Let us be conjunctive in our revenge

against him: if thou canst cuckold him, thou dost
thyself a pleasure, me a sport. There are many
events in the womb of time which will be delivered.
Traverse! go, provide thy money. We will have more
of this to-morrow. Adieu.

RODERIGO
Where shall we meet i' the morning?

IAGO
At my lodging.

RODERIGO
I'll be with thee betimes.

IAGO
Go to; farewell. Do you hear, Roderigo?

RODERIGO
What say you?

IAGO
No more of drowning, do you hear?

RODERIGO

in a better way than drowning yourself. Make as much money
as you can: religious vows and weak promises between
a barbarian and a tricky Venetian girl are not too difficult for me to take advantage of. If I do well, you
will sleep with her, so make money. And stop talking
of drowning! It is beside the point. Instead try to get hanged by committing wrongs in order to be with her,
than to drown and be without her.

Can I trust you while I see what happens?

Yes. Now go, make money. I have told you over and over: I
hate the Moor. I have good reason to help you, just
as you do. Let us join together to take our revenge
on him and make it so you sleep with his wife, which will be a great pleasure to me. Many things must happen next.
Now go! make more money. We will talk more tomorrow. Goodbye.

Where shall we meet tomorrow morning?

At my house.

I'll be there early.

Good, goodbye. Oh, and Roderigo?

Yes, Iago?

Stop talking of drowning, alright?

I am changed: I'll go sell all my land.

Exit

IAGO
Thus do I ever make my fool my purse:
For I mine own gain'd knowledge should profane,
If I would time expend with such a snipe.
But for my sport and profit. I hate the Moor:

And it is thought abroad, that 'twixt my sheets
He has done my office: I know not if't be true;
But I, for mere suspicion in that kind,
Will do as if for surety. He holds me well;
The better shall my purpose work on him.
Cassio's a proper man: let me see now:

To get his place and to plume up my will
In double knavery--How, how? Let's see:--
After some time, to abuse Othello's ear
That he is too familiar with his wife.
He hath a person and a smooth dispose
To be suspected, framed to make women false.

The Moor is of a free and open nature,
That thinks men honest that but seem to be so,

And will as tenderly be led by the nose
As asses are.
I have't. It is engender'd. Hell and night
Must bring this monstrous birth to the world's light.
Exit

Yes, I have changed my mind. I will sell my land for money.

*And that is how I use fools for money.
If I didn't have my own gain to get out of it,
I would never spend time with such a fool.
But he helps me get money and achieve my purposes: I hate the Moor,
And there is a rumor that he has slept
With my wife. I don't know if that is true,
But just because of the rumor I
Will act as if it is. He thinks highly of me,
Which will make it easier for me to trick him.
Now then, let me see: Cassio is a good and handsome man.
How can I get his rank and hurt Othello
At the same time? How?
After a little while, I will tell Othello
That Cassio is too close to Desdemona.
His personality and smooth disposition
Can easily be suspected, they already make him look like a seducer.
The Moor is a straightforward man
Who thinks other men are honest if they look honest enough,
And so he can be led on as easily
As donkeys are.
I know what I will do. Hell and the devil
Will help me work out my plans.*

Act II

Scene I. A Sea-port in Cyprus. An open place near the quay.

Enter MONTANO and two Gentlemen

MONTANO
What from the cape can you discern at sea?

What do you see out in the ocean?

First Gentleman
Nothing at all: it is a highwrought flood;
I cannot, 'twixt the heaven and the main,

*Nothing. The water is so rough
That I cannot see between the ocean and heaven*

Descry a sail.

A single sail.

MONTANO
Methinks the wind hath spoke aloud at land;
A fuller blast ne'er shook our battlements:
If it hath ruffian'd so upon the sea,
What ribs of oak, when mountains melt on them,

*It is windy here on the land as well.
A gust shook our fortifications:
If it is so strong out on the sea,
Why wooden whip, when mountains of water fall on them,*

Can hold the mortise? What shall we hear of this?

Can stay together? What is going to happen?

Second Gentleman
A segregation of the Turkish fleet:
For do but stand upon the foaming shore,
The chidden billow seems to pelt the clouds;

*The Turkish fleet will be broken up.
Standing here on the shore,
The waves look like they will hit the clouds.*

The wind-shaked surge, with high and monstrous mane,

The surge of water powered by the winds, rising high,

Seems to cast water on the burning bear,

Seems to throw water to the constellations

And quench the guards of the ever-fixed pole:
I never did like molestation view
On the enchafed flood.

*And drench the polestars.
I have never seen such a storm
Out on the sea.*

MONTANO
If that the Turkish fleet
Be not enshelter'd and embay'd, they are drown'd:

*If the Turkish ships
Do not find shelter and rest, they will be sunk.*

It is impossible they bear it out.

It is impossible for them to withstand this.

Enter a third Gentleman

Third Gentleman
News, lads! our wars are done.
The desperate tempest hath so bang'd the Turks,

*I have news! The fighting is done.
The storm has injured the Turks so much*

That their designment halts: a noble ship of Venice

That they have stopped their plans. A ship from Venice

Hath seen a grievous wreck and sufferance

On most part of their fleet.

MONTANO
How! is this true?

Third Gentleman
The ship is here put in,
A Veronesa; Michael Cassio,
Lieutenant to the warlike Moor Othello,
Is come on shore: the Moor himself at sea,
And is in full commission here for Cyprus.

MONTANO
I am glad on't; 'tis a worthy governor.

Third Gentleman
But this same Cassio, though he speak of comfort

Touching the Turkish loss, yet he looks sadly,
And prays the Moor be safe; for they were parted

With foul and violent tempest.

MONTANO
Pray heavens he be;
For I have served him, and the man commands
Like a full soldier. Let's to the seaside, ho!
As well to see the vessel that's come in
As to throw out our eyes for brave Othello,
Even till we make the main and the aerial blue
An indistinct regard.

Third Gentleman
Come, let's do so:
For every minute is expectancy
Of more arrivance.
Enter CASSIO

CASSIO
Thanks, you the valiant of this warlike isle,

That so approve the Moor! O, let the heavens

Give him defence against the elements,
For I have lost us him on a dangerous sea.

MONTANO
Is he well shipp'd?

Has seen an awful wreck of theirs and the sufferings
Of most of their fleet.

What! Is this true!

The ship has just landed,
From Verona. Michael Cassio,
Lieutenant to the Moor general Othello,
Is on the shore. The Moor himself is at sea
And is coming with full commission to Cyprus.

I am glad, he is a worthy leader.

But this Cassio fellow, though he has good news
About the Turkish losses, is sad
And prays for the Moor's safety. They were separated
In the storm.

Yes, I pray he is safe.
I have served under him and he leads
Like a great soldier. Let us go to the shore.
See to the vessel that has arrived and
Look for brave Othello
Until the sea and sky blur together
And are indistinguishable.

Come, let's go.
Every minute we can expect
Their arrival.

Thank you, you brave men who defend the island
And respect the Moor! O, I pray that the heavens
Defend him against the storm,
For we were separated on the dangerous sea.

Is his ship strong?

CASSIO
His bark is stoutly timber'd, his pilot

Of very expert and approved allowance;
Therefore my hopes, not surfeited to death,
Stand in bold cure.
A cry within 'A sail, a sail, a sail!'
Enter a fourth Gentleman

The wood is good and strong, and his pilot
Is experienced – a true expert.
Therefore, I hope for his safety, though
They are not without their fears.

CASSIO
What noise?

What is that sound?

Fourth Gentleman
The town is empty; on the brow o' the sea
Stand ranks of people, and they cry 'A sail!'

The whole town is at the shore
Standing in lines and shouting that
they see a sail!

CASSIO
My hopes do shape him for the governor.
Guns heard

I hope it is Othello.

Second Gentlemen
They do discharge their shot of courtesy:
Our friends at least.

They have fired a friendly shot,
So they are at least our allies.

CASSIO
I pray you, sir, go forth,
And give us truth who 'tis that is arrived.

Please, sir, go
And tell us who it is who is arriving.

Second Gentleman
I shall.
Exit

I will.

MONTANO
But, good lieutenant, is your general wived?

Good lieutenant, does the general have
a wife?

CASSIO
Most fortunately: he hath achieved a maid

That paragons description and wild fame;

One that excels the quirks of blazoning pens,
And in the essential vesture of creation

Does tire the ingener.
Re-enter second Gentleman

Yes, and he is very lucky. His wife's
virtues
Cannot be described or become
famous enough to match them.
She is no match for a writer who,
In trying to capture her, God's special
creation,
Will become tired.

How now! who has put in?

Hello, who is it that has arrive?

Second Gentleman
'Tis one Iago, ancient to the general.

It is one named Iago, ensign to the
general.

CASSIO
Has had most favourable and happy speed:
Tempests themselves, high seas, and howling winds,
The gutter'd rocks and congregated sands--
Traitors ensteep'd to clog the guiltless keel,--
As having sense of beauty, do omit
Their mortal natures, letting go safely by
The divine Desdemona.

He has come very quickly.
Storms and high seas and howling winds,
And the dangerous rocks and swirling sands –
Everything that will slow and stop a ship –
Must have a sense of beauty, for they
Have acted against their natures and allowed
The beautiful Desdemona to travel safely.

MONTANO
What is she?

Who is Desdemona?

CASSIO
She that I spake of, our great captain's captain,
Left in the conduct of the bold Iago,
Whose footing here anticipates our thoughts
A se'nnight's speed. Great Jove, Othello guard,

And swell his sail with thine own powerful breath,

That he may bless this bay with his tall ship,
Make love's quick pants in Desdemona's arms,
Give renew'd fire to our extinct spirits
And bring all Cyprus comfort!
*Enter DESDEMONA, EMILIA, IAGO, RODERIGO,
and Attendants*

She is whom I spoke of, the wife of Othello,
Given to brave Iago's care,
And he has arrive here
A week earlier than expected. Dear God,
protect Othello
And make his ship sail faster with your breath
pushing it
That he might arrive here in his great ship,
Be joined in love with Desdemona,
Replenish the fire of our spirits,
And bring all of Cyprus comfort!

O, behold,
The riches of the ship is come on shore!

Behold,
*The riches from the ship have come onto the
shore!*

Ye men of Cyprus, let her have your knees.
Hail to thee, lady! and the grace of heaven,
Before, behind thee, and on every hand,
Enwheel thee round!

Men of Cyprus, bow to her.
Hello, lady! May the grace of heaven
Be before you, behind you, on each side,
All around you!

DESDEMONA
I thank you, valiant Cassio.
What tidings can you tell me of my lord?

Thank you, brave Cassio.
How is Othello doing?

CASSIO
He is not yet arrived: nor know I aught

But that he's well and will be shortly here.

*He has not arrived yet, so I don't know
anything*
Except that he is fine and will soon be here.

DESDEMONA
O, but I fear--How lost you company?

*O, but I am scared. How did you get
separated?*

CASSIO
The great contention of the sea and skies
Parted our fellowship--But, hark! a sail.

The great storm of the sea and skies
Parted us. But wait! a sail.

Within 'A sail, a sail!' Guns heard

Second Gentleman
They give their greeting to the citadel;
This likewise is a friend.

> *Another greeting shot to the city:*
> *This is also an ally.*

CASSIO
See for the news.
Exit Gentleman
Good ancient, you are welcome.
To EMILIA
Welcome, mistress.
Let it not gall your patience, good Iago,

That I extend my manners; 'tis my breeding

That gives me this bold show of courtesy.

Kissing her

> *See who it is.*
>
> *Good ensign, you are welcome here.*
>
> *And mistress, welcome.*
> *I hope this does not offend you, good Iago,*
> *That I greet your wife like this. I have been raised*
> *To give such a bold custom of greeting.*

IAGO
Sir, would she give you so much of her lips
As of her tongue she oft bestows on me,
You'll have enough.

> *Sir, if she gives you as much of her lips*
> *As she gives me by berating me,*
> *You'll be sick of her.*

DESDEMONA
Alas, she has no speech.

> *No, she seems to say nothing.*

IAGO
In faith, too much;
I find it still, when I have list to sleep:
Marry, before your ladyship, I grant,
She puts her tongue a little in her heart,
And chides with thinking.

> *Truly, she says too much,*
> *Even when I am trying to sleep.*
> *Yes, in front of you, I agree*
> *She says very little, but in her heart*
> *She is speaking scornfully to me.*

EMILIA
You have little cause to say so.

> *You have no reason to say that.*

IAGO
Come on, come on; you are pictures out of doors,

Bells in your parlors, wild-cats in your kitchens,

Saints in your injuries, devils being offended,

Players in your housewifery, and housewives' in your beds.

> *Come on now. Out in public you women are pretty as a picture,*
> *But you are loud bells at home, wildcats in the kitchen,*
>
> *Saints when injured, devils when offended,*
> *Idle actresses in your housewife duties and hussies in your bed.*

DESDEMONA
O, fie upon thee, slanderer!

> *O, a curse on you, you slanderer.*

IAGO
Nay, it is true, or else I am a Turk:
You rise to play and go to bed to work.

No, I would be a Turk if what I say is not true.
You get up in order to enjoy yourselves, and
you go to bed in order to work.

EMILIA
You shall not write my praise.

You will not say anything good about me.

IAGO
No, let me not.

No, I won't.

DESDEMONA
What wouldst thou write of me, if thou shouldst
praise me?

What verse would you write of me if you had
to say something nice?

IAGO
O gentle lady, do not put me to't;
For I am nothing, if not critical.

Gentle lady, do not make me do that.
I am a critical person by nature.

DESDEMONA
Come on assay. There's one gone to the harbour?

Come on, try. And has someone gone to the
harbor?

IAGO
Ay, madam.

Yes, madam.

DESDEMONA
I am not merry; but I do beguile

The thing I am, by seeming otherwise.

Come, how wouldst thou praise me?

I am not really this playful, but I don't want to
show
How I really am by seeming other than
playful.
Come on, how would you praise me?

IAGO
I am about it; but indeed my invention
Comes from my pate as birdlime does from frize;

It plucks out brains and all: but my Muse labours,

And thus she is deliver'd.
If she be fair and wise, fairness and wit,
The one's for use, the other useth it.

I am thinking, but creative verse
Comes from my head as difficultly as sticky
birdlime comes out of wool cloth.
It takes all of my brains. But my Muse has
worked at it,
And I have something:
"If a woman has beauty and intelligence,
She uses her beauty to get what she wants,
and uses it as a tool of her intelligence."

DESDEMONA
Well praised! How if she be black and witty?

Well said! But what if she is ugly and smart?

IAGO
If she be black, and thereto have a wit,

She'll find a white that shall her blackness fit.

"If she is ugly, but still have brains,

She will trick some handsome man to love her
ugliness."

DESDEMONA
Worse and worse.

This is getting even worse.

EMILIA
How if fair and foolish?

IAGO
She never yet was foolish that was fair;
For even her folly help'd her to an heir.

DESDEMONA
These are old fond paradoxes to make fools laugh i'

the alehouse. What miserable praise hast thou for

her that's foul and foolish?

IAGO
There's none so foul and foolish thereunto,

But does foul pranks which fair and wise ones do.

DESDEMONA
O heavy ignorance! thou praisest the worst best.

But what praise couldst thou bestow on a deserving

woman indeed, one that, in the authority of her
merit, did justly put on the vouch of very malice itself?

IAGO
She that was ever fair and never proud,

Had tongue at will and yet was never loud,
Never lack'd gold and yet went never gay,

Fled from her wish and yet said 'Now I may,'

She that being anger'd, her revenge being nigh,
Bade her wrong stay and her displeasure fly,

She that in wisdom never was so frail

To change the cod's head for the salmon's tail;

She that could think and ne'er disclose her mind,

See suitors following and not look behind,

She was a wight, if ever such wight were,--

What if she is beautiful and dumb?

*"No beautiful woman was ever dumb,
Because even her foolishness makes
her seem attractive."*

*These are old jokes intended for laughs in
the tavern. What awful things do you have to say
About the woman who is ugly and dumb?*

*"No matter how dumb and ugly a woman is,
She tricks men just like the beautiful and smart ones do."*

*O you are so ignorant! You praise the worst combination most!
But what would you say about a very good woman,
one that, based on her own
good merit, can have nothing bad said of her?*

*"She who was beautiful but never proud,
Could speak well but was never loud,
Always looked good, but not ostentatious,
Who could get what she wanted, but chose against it,
Who when angry was not revengeful,
And overlooked it when people wronged her,
She whose wisdom is not so weak that she would
Mix up the head of a codfish with the tail of a salmon,
She who can think but doesnt need to reveal her thoughts,
Who sees suitors following after her but does not look behind at them,
She is a woman, if ever such a woman existed–*

DESDEMONA
To do what?

And what would she do?

IAGO
To suckle fools and chronicle small beer.

She would raise children, and keep track of trifles.

DESDEMONA
O most lame and impotent conclusion! Do not learn of him, Emilia, though he be thy husband. How say you, Cassio? is he not a most profane and liberal counsellor?

O what a pathetic ending! Do not listen to him, Emilia, even if he is your husband. What do you think, Cassio? Isn't he the rudest teacher?

CASSIO
He speaks home, madam: You may relish him more in

the soldier than in the scholar.

He speaks commonly, madam. You will find more worth in him
as a soldier than as a scholar.

IAGO
[Aside] He takes her by the palm: ay, well said, whisper: with as little a web as this will I ensnare as great a fly as Cassio. Ay, smile upon

her, do; I will gyve thee in thine own courtship. You say true; 'tis so, indeed: if such tricks as these strip you out of your lieutenantry, it had

been better you had not kissed your three fingers so oft, which now again you are most apt to play the sir in. Very good; well kissed! an excellent courtesy! 'tis so, indeed. Yet again your fingers

to your lips? would they were clyster-pipes for your sake!

He holds her hand. Yes, good, whisper together. This itself is enough for me to use Cassio for my plans. Good, smile
at her. Your manners will help me bind you. You speak truly of your manners: if they will be used to take your rank away from you, maybe you should
not have done such polite mannerisms so often, which you are very good at doing. Very good, kiss her! A wonderful gesture indeed. And again you place your fingers
to your lips? If only they were enema tubes to clean out your crap!

Trumpet within
The Moor! I know his trumpet.

That's the Moor; I recognize his trumpet!

CASSIO
'Tis truly so.

It's true.

DESDEMONA
Let's meet him and receive him.

Let's go meet him.

CASSIO
Lo, where he comes!
Enter OTHELLO and Attendants

There he is, coming to us.

OTHELLO
O my fair warrior!

O my beautiful warrior!

DESDEMONA
My dear Othello!

My dear Othello!

OTHELLO
It gives me wonder great as my content
To see you here before me. O my soul's joy!

If after every tempest come such calms,
May the winds blow till they have waken'd death!

And let the labouring bark climb hills of seas
Olympus-high and duck again as low

As hell's from heaven! If it were now to die,

'Twere now to be most happy; for, I fear,
My soul hath her content so absolute
That not another comfort like to this
Succeeds in unknown fate.

DESDEMONA
The heavens forbid
But that our loves and comforts should increase,
Even as our days do grow!

OTHELLO
Amen to that, sweet powers!
I cannot speak enough of this content;

It stops me here; it is too much of joy:

And this, and this, the greatest discords

Kissing her
That e'er our hearts shall make!

IAGO
[Aside] O, you are well tuned now!
But I'll set down the pegs that make this music,
As honest as I am.

OTHELLO
Come, let us to the castle.
News, friends; our wars are done, the Turks are drown'd.

How does my old acquaintance of this isle?
Honey, you shall be well desired in Cyprus;

I have found great love amongst them. O my sweet,

I prattle out of fashion, and I dote

In mine own comforts. I prithee, good Iago,
Go to the bay and disembark my coffers:

I am amazed as well as happy
To see you here before I arrived. O
joy!
If every storm had after it such calms,
Then the winds should blow so hard
that they wake the dead!
Let the ships ride the high waves,
As high as Mt. Olympus, and duck low
again,
As far as hell is from heaven! If I died
now,
I would die most happy, for I fear
That since I am so completely content,
No comfort will come close to this
In my lifetime.

I pray to God
That our love and comfort increases
As we grow older!

Amen to that!
I cannot say anything more about my
happiness,
It forces me to stop speaking because
it is too much to comprehend.
And I hope this kiss is the greatest
fight

That we ever face!

O, you are in good spirits now!
I'll bring you down from this height,
Since I am the honest man.

Come, let's go to the castle.
Friends, our fighting is over; the Turks
have drowned.
How are my old friends on the island?
Honey, you will be loved here in
Cyprus;
I myself have been treated well here. O
my sweet,
I am talking nonsense and I am
obsessing
Over my happiness. Please, good Iago,
Go to the bay and get me things,

Bring thou the master to the citadel;
He is a good one, and his worthiness
Does challenge much respect. Come, Desdemona,

Once more, well met at Cyprus.

Exeunt OTHELLO, DESDEMONA, and Attendants

IAGO
Do thou meet me presently at the harbour. Come
hither. If thou be'st valiant,-- as, they say, base
men being in love have then a nobility in their
natures more than is native to them--list me. The
lieutenant tonight watches on the court of
guard:--first, I must tell thee this--Desdemona is
directly in love with him.

RODERIGO
With him! why, 'tis not possible.

IAGO
Lay thy finger thus, and let thy soul be instructed.
Mark me with what violence she first loved the Moor,

but for bragging and telling her fantastical lies:
and will she love him still for prating? let not

thy discreet heart think it. Her eye must be fed;

and what delight shall she have to look on the

devil? When the blood is made dull with the act of
sport, there should be, again to inflame it and to
give satiety a fresh appetite, loveliness in favour,

sympathy in years, manners and beauties; all which
the Moor is defective in: now, for want of these

required conveniences, her delicate tenderness will

find itself abused, begin to heave the gorge,
disrelish and abhor the Moor; very nature will
instruct her in it and compel her to some second

choice. Now, sir, this granted,--as it is a most
pregnant and unforced position--who stands so
eminent in the degree of this fortune as Cassio
does? a knave very voluble; no further
conscionable than in putting on the mere form of

civil and humane seeming, for the better compassing

---

*And bring the captain of the ship to the castle.
He is a good soldier, and his worth
Makes me respect him greatly. Come,
Desdemona,
I'll say it again, I am happy to see you at
Cyprus!*

*Meet me at the harbor now. Come
on. If you are brave – as they say, evil
men in love have a nobility and braveness
that is not naturally in them – listen to me.
Cassio is tasked tonight with
guard duty, and I must tell you: Desdemona is
in love with him.*

With him! That's not possible.

*Be quiet and listen to what I will tell you.
Look at how quickly and impulsively sh fell in
love for the Moor,
from his bragging and tall tales,
do you think she will keep loving him as he
speaks nonsense? Don't
be stupid enough to think so. She needs
someone handsome
and how could she possibly enjoy looking at
that
devil? In time, the heat of romance goes away,
and one needs certain things to reignite it and
recreate sexual appetite, like handsomeness
and
similarity in age, customs, and appearance.
The Moor has none of these. Since she has
none
of these necessary qualities in her partner, she
will feel
sick of him, to the point of puking,
and will disgust the Moor. Her nature will
cause this disgust and then turn her to look for
a second
option. Now since this is true – it's a very
natural string of events – who would be
a better second option for her than Cassio?
After all, he is a very smooth speaker,
a trait that makes him seem conscientious, as
if he is
polite and civil, but in reality it hides*

of his salt and most hidden loose affection? why,
none; why, none: a slipper and subtle knave, a

finder of occasions, that has an eye can stamp and

counterfeit advantages, though true advantage never

present itself; a devilish knave. Besides, the

knave is handsome, young, and hath all those
requisites in him that folly and green minds look
after: a pestilent complete knave; and the woman

hath found him already.

RODERIGO
I cannot believe that in her; she's full of
most blessed condition.

IAGO
Blessed fig's-end! the wine she drinks is made of
grapes: if she had been blessed, she would never

have loved the Moor. Blessed pudding! Didst thou
not see her paddle with the palm of his hand? Didst
not mark that?

RODERIGO
Yes, that I did; but that was but courtesy.

IAGO
Lechery, by this hand; an index and obscure prologue
to the history of lust and foul thoughts. They met

so near with their lips that their breaths embraced

together. Villanous thoughts, Roderigo! when these
mutualities so marshal the way, hard at hand comes

the master and main exercise, the incorporate
conclusion, Pish! But, sir, be you ruled by me: I

have brought you from Venice. Watch you to-night;

for the command, I'll lay't upon you. Cassio knows

you not. I'll not be far from you: do you find
some occasion to anger Cassio, either by speaking

too loud, or tainting his discipline; or from what

his inner, strong lustfulness.
No one stands in a better position, and no one
is trickier than he is,
a man who finds the right time for his moves,
who sees
and creates his own advantageous situations
even if a real advantage
is never there – he is a devilish trickster.
Besides,
he is handsome and young, with all of the
qualities that naive youths look for.
He is an awful man, but seems the perfect one,
and Desdemona
has already fallen for him.

I do not believe it. She is a very
moral and trustworthy woman.

Nonsense! She drinks the same wine we do,
made of grapes – she has the same desires we
do. If she was blessedly moral, she never
would have loved the Moor. Didn't you
see her fondle Cassio's hands? Didn't you
notice?

Yes, but that was just politeness.

It was lust, and it foreshadows
a future of lust and impure thoughts between
them. They came
so close to each others lips that their breaths
hugged.
Evil thoughts, Roderigo! When two
people mutually act like this, quickly will
come
the main goal of their actions, the obvious
onclusion, which is sex. But, Roderigo, listen
to me: I
brought you here from Venice. Keep watch
tonight
and I will give you the sign to act. Cassio
doesn't know
you. I will be nearby: you must find
some way to make Cassio angry, either by
speaking
obnoxiously, or insulting him, or however

other course you please, which the time shall more
favourably minister.

RODERIGO
Well.

IAGO
Sir, he is rash and very sudden in choler, and haply
may strike at you: provoke him, that he may; for
even out of that will I cause these of Cyprus to

mutiny; whose qualification shall come into no true

taste again but by the displanting of Cassio. So

shall you have a shorter journey to your desires by

the means I shall then have to prefer them; and the
impediment most profitably removed, without the

which there were no expectation of our prosperity.

RODERIGO
I will do this, if I can bring it to any opportunity.

IAGO
I warrant thee. Meet me by and by at the citadel:
I must fetch his necessaries ashore. Farewell.

RODERIGO
Adieu.
Exit

IAGO
That Cassio loves her, I do well believe it;
That she loves him, 'tis apt and of great credit:

The Moor, howbeit that I endure him not,
Is of a constant, loving, noble nature,
And I dare think he'll prove to Desdemona
A most dear husband. Now, I do love her too;

Not out of absolute lust, though peradventure
I stand accountant for as great a sin,
But partly led to diet my revenge,
For that I do suspect the lusty Moor
Hath leap'd into my seat; the thought whereof
Doth, like a poisonous mineral, gnaw my inwards;
And nothing can or shall content my soul
Till I am even'd with him, wife for wife,

---

you want according to the situation.

Fine.

Sir, he has a poor temper and angers easily,
he may try to hit you. Try to get him to do that
and from that simple action I will cause
Cyprus to
mutiny against him so that they will not
become
peaceful until Cassio is removed from his
post. Thus,
you will have an easier path to your desire for
Desdemona by
these means which will
remove your biggest obstacle. If it is not
removed,
then there is no hope of succeeding.

I will do this as long as it gives me a chance.

I promise you. Meet me soon at the castle;
I must get Othello's things from the ship.
Goodbye

Goodbye.

I actually think Cassio does love her,
And it makes sense that she would love him as
well.
The Moor whom I can't stand
Is such an honest, loving, noble man
And I think he will be to Desdemona
A very good husband. I love Desdemona as
well,
Though not from lust as much as from
Needing to get even with the Moor.
I want to get revenge
Since I think that the lustful Moor
Slept with my wife – this thought,
Like a poison, eats at me inside.
Nothing can or will make me feel better
Until I am even with him, wife for wife,

Or failing so, yet that I put the Moor

At least into a jealousy so strong
That judgment cannot cure. Which thing to do,
If this poor trash of Venice, whom I trash
For his quick hunting, stand the putting on,
I'll have our Michael Cassio on the hip,
Abuse him to the Moor in the rank garb--
For I fear Cassio with my night-cap too--

Make the Moor thank me, love me and reward me

For making him egregiously an ass
And practising upon his peace and quiet
Even to madness. 'Tis here, but yet confused:

Knavery's plain face is never seen till used.

Exit

Or, if I fail to do that, I will at least make the Moor
So extremely jealous
That he won't be able to think properly.
If I can make Roderigo, that Venetian trash,
Do whatever I need him to do,
I will have control over Cassio
And will defame him to the Moor –
After all, I am afraid Cassio might have slept with my wife as well –
And by doing this the Moor will thank me, love me, and reward me,
All for making a fool of him
And removing his peace and quietness,
Replacing it with madness. Everything is here that I need, just not perfectly planned yet.
I never fully know a trick until the moment when it is put into action.

Scene II. A street.

Enter a Herald with a proclamation; People following

Herald
It is Othello's pleasure, our noble and valiant
general, that, upon certain tidings now arrived,
importing the mere perdition of the Turkish fleet,
every man put himself into triumph; some to dance,
some to make bonfires, each man to what sport and
revels his addiction leads him: for, besides these
beneficial news, it is the celebration of his
nuptial. So much was his pleasure should be
proclaimed. All offices are open, and there is full
liberty of feasting from this present hour of five
till the bell have told eleven. Heaven bless the
isle of Cyprus and our noble general Othello!

Exeunt

*It is the order of Othelle, the brave and noble
general, that since we now have new
of the destruction of the Turkish fleet,
everyone should celebrate, and dance,
and make bonfires, each person to whatever
fun and partying he wants. On top of this
great news, we will celebrate Othello's
wedding. That was the entirety of his
announcement. There will be a full
feast from now, five o'clock,
until the bell tolls eleven. God bless the
island of Cyprus and our brave general
Othello!*

Scene III. A hall in the castle.

Enter OTHELLO, DESDEMONA, CASSIO, and Attendants

OTHELLO
Good Michael, look you to the guard to-night:
Let's teach ourselves that honourable stop,
Not to outsport discretion.

Good Michael Cassio, keep the guard tonight
And help the festivities show restraint,
And not get out of control.

CASSIO
Iago hath direction what to do;
But, notwithstanding, with my personal eye
Will I look to't.

Iago has instructions on what to do.
But, regardless, I will personally
Look after it.

OTHELLO
Iago is most honest.
Michael, good night: to-morrow with your earliest
Let me have speech with you.
To DESDEMONA
Come, my dear love,
The purchase made, the fruits are to ensue;

That profit's yet to come 'tween me and you.

Good night.
Exeunt OTHELLO, DESDEMONA, and Attendants
Enter IAGO

Iago is very honest.
Michael, goodnight. Early tomorrow
I would like to talk with you.

Come, my love,
The purchase of marrying you has been made,
the fruits of sex are to come next.
That pleasure hasn't happened yet, but is next
for us.
Goodnight.

CASSIO
Welcome, Iago; we must to the watch.

Welcome, Iago, let's go to keep watch.

IAGO
Not this hour, lieutenant; 'tis not yet ten o' the
clock. Our general cast us thus early for the love

of his Desdemona; who let us not therefore blame:
he hath not yet made wanton the night with her; and
she is sport for Jove.

Not yet, lieutenant. It's not yet ten o' clock.
Our general mades us leave early because of
his love
for Desdemona. We can't blame him though:
he hasn't yet slept with her, and
she is beautiful enough for Jove to love her.

CASSIO
She's a most exquisite lady.

She is a beautiful lady.

IAGO
And, I'll warrant her, fun of game.

And, I'll bet, very good in bed.

CASSIO
Indeed, she's a most fresh and delicate creature.

Yes, she's very young and delicate.

IAGO
What an eye she has! methinks it sounds a parley

And what beautiful eyes! They are almost

of provocation.

provocatively inviting.

CASSIO
An inviting eye; and yet methinks right modest.

Inviting, yes, but I think she is still appropriately modest.

IAGO
And when she speaks, is it not an alarum to love?

And isn't her voice a beautiful bell?

CASSIO
She is indeed perfection.

She is quite perfect.

IAGO
Well, happiness to their sheets! Come, lieutenant,

I have a stoup of wine; and here without are a brace
of Cyprus gallants that would fain have a measure
to the health of black Othello.

*Well, I wish their marriage bed happiness! Come, lieutenant, I
have a bottle of wine, and here is a group
of Cyprus gentlemen who would love to drink to
black Othello's health.*

CASSIO
Not to-night, good Iago: I have very poor and
unhappy brains for drinking: I could well wish
courtesy would invent some other custom of
entertainment.

*Not tonight, good Iago: I have very poor
tolerance for alcohol. I wish
that society would invent some other way
to celebrate.*

IAGO
O, they are our friends; but one cup: I'll drink for
you.

*But these are friends. Drink one cup, I'll drink the
rest for you.*

CASSIO
I have drunk but one cup to-night, and that was
craftily qualified too, and, behold, what innovation
it makes here: I am unfortunate in the infirmity,

and dare not task my weakness with any more.

*I have already had a cup tonight, and even that
was watered down, and yet look at how drunk
it has made me. I have an unfortunately weak
tolerance,
and wouldn't want to test my weakness by drinking
more.*

IAGO
What, man! 'tis a night of revels: the gallants
desire it.

*You can't be serious! Tonight is a night of partying,
and the gentlemen want you to drink*

CASSIO
Where are they?

Where are they?

IAGO
Here at the door; I pray you, call them in.

Just outside the door. Please, ask them to come in.

CASSIO
I'll do't; but it dislikes me.

I'll do it, but I don't want to.

Exit

IAGO
If I can fasten but one cup upon him,
With that which he hath drunk to-night already,
He'll be as full of quarrel and offence

As my young mistress' dog. Now, my sick fool
Roderigo,
Whom love hath turn'd almost the wrong side out,
To Desdemona hath to-night caroused
Potations pottle-deep; and he's to watch:

Three lads of Cyprus, noble swelling spirits,
That hold their honours in a wary distance,
The very elements of this warlike isle,
Have I to-night fluster'd with flowing cups,
And they watch too. Now, 'mongst this flock of
drunkards,
Am I to put our Cassio in some action
That may offend the isle.--But here they come:
If consequence do but approve my dream,

My boat sails freely, both with wind and stream.

*Re-enter CASSIO; with him MONTANO and Gentlemen;
servants following with wine*

CASSIO
'Fore God, they have given me a rouse already.

MONTANO
Good faith, a little one; not past a pint, as I am
a soldier.

IAGO
Some wine, ho!
Sings
And let me the canakin clink, clink;
And let me the canakin clink
A soldier's a man;
A life's but a span;
Why, then, let a soldier drink.
Some wine, boys!

CASSIO
'Fore God, an excellent song.

IAGO
I learned it in England, where, indeed, they are
most potent in potting: your Dane, your German,

If I can make him drink only one cup more
On top of what he has already drunk tonight,
Then he will be as aggressive and ready to
fight
As my mistress's dog. Now, my lovesick fool
Roderigo,
Whom love has twisted up and confused,
Has drunk tonight to Desdemona
In a number of toasts, and he's on guard duty
as well.
Three Cyprus men, brave spirits
That have a good notion of their honor
Like everyone on this warring island,
I have also gotten drunk,
And they are on duty as well. Now, with this
group of drunkards –
I need to get Cassio to do something
To offend their island. Here they come:
If I can engineer this situation to match my
plans,
Then I will get what I want.

By God, they have already given me quite a
lot to drink.

Truly, only a small cup. It wasn't even a pint,
I promise as a soldier.

More wine!

And clink your glasses together
And clink your glasses together
A soldier is a man,
And a life is only so long,
So let the soldier drink!
More wine, boys!

By God, a great song.

I learned it in England, where they are
very good at drinking. The Dane, or German,
or

and your swag-bellied Hollander--Drink, ho!--are to your English.

fat Dutchman – Drink! – they are no match to the English.

CASSIO
Is your Englishman so expert in his drinking?

Is the Englishman truly an expert at drinking?

IAGO
Why, he drinks you, with facility, your Dane dead drunk; he sweats not to overthrow your Almain; he gives your Hollander a vomit, ere the next pottle can be filled.

Why, he will easily drink a Dane into a stupor, he has no problem outdrinking the German, and he will make a Dutchman pute before the next glass can be filled.

CASSIO
To the health of our general!

To the health of Othello!

MONTANO
I am for it, lieutenant; and I'll do you justice.

I will drink to that, lieutenant, as much as you will.

IAGO
O sweet England!
King Stephen was a worthy peer,
His breeches cost him but a crown;
He held them sixpence all too dear,
With that he call'd the tailor lown.
He was a wight of high renown,
And thou art but of low degree:
'Tis pride that pulls the country down;
Then take thine auld cloak about thee.
Some wine, ho!

O sweet England!
King Stephen was a good king,
And his pants were very cheap.
He thought he spent sixpence too much
And called his tailor a rascal.
He was a man of great reputation,
And you are a man of low rank:
It's pride that destroys the country,
So be happy with your old cloak
More wine!

CASSIO
Why, this is a more exquisite song than the other.

Why, that is an even better song than the last one.

IAGO
Will you hear't again?

Would you like me to sing it again?

CASSIO
No; for I hold him to be unworthy of his place that does those things. Well, God's above all; and there be souls must be saved, and there be souls must not be saved.

No, I don't think it is right for us to be doing those things. Well, God's in charge, and there must be some souls that get saved, and some that don't

IAGO
It's true, good lieutenant.

Very true, lieutenant.

CASSIO
For mine own part,--no offence to the general, nor any man of quality,--I hope to be saved.

For me – and no offense to the general or anyone else – I hope I am saved.

IAGO
And so do I too, lieutenant.

As do I, lieutenant.

CASSIO
Ay, but, by your leave, not before me; the
lieutenant is to be saved before the ancient. Let's

have no more of this; let's to our affairs.—Forgive
us our sins!--Gentlemen, let's look to our business.
Do not think, gentlemen, I am drunk: this is my

ancient; this is my right hand, and this is my left:

. I am not drunk now; I can stand well enough, and
speak well enough.

All
Excellent well.

CASSIO
Why, very well then; you must not think then that I
am drunk.
Exit

MONTANO
To the platform, masters; come, let's set the watch.

IAGO
You see this fellow that is gone before;
He is a soldier fit to stand by Caesar

And give direction: and do but see his vice;
'Tis to his virtue a just equinox,
The one as long as the other: 'tis pity of him.
I fear the trust Othello puts him in
On some odd time of his infirmity,
Will shake this island.

MONTANO
But is he often thus?

IAGO
'Tis evermore the prologue to his sleep:
He'll watch the horologe a double set,
If drink rock not his cradle.

MONTANO
It were well
The general were put in mind of it.
Perhaps he sees it not; or his good nature
Prizes the virtue that appears in Cassio,
And looks not on his evils: is not this true?
Enter RODERIGO

*Yes, but please, not before me. The
lieutenant must be saved before the ensign.
But
no more of this, let's go to the watch. Forgive
us our sins! Gentlemen, let's do our work.
Do not think, men, that I am drunk. Look: this
is my
ensign, this is my right hand, this is my left
hand –
you can see I am not drunk. I can stand and
speak well enough.*

Yes, very well.

Yes, very well. You must not think I am drunk.

*Let's go to the platform, everyone, and get to
the watch.*

*You see that man who just left?
He is a good enough soldier to stand next to
Caesar
And give orders, but you see his vice,
Which is an extreme opposite to his virtue.
The one is as great as the other, it's too bad.
I am afraid that Othello trusts him too much
And that at some time this weakness
Will be bad for the island.*

Is he often this drunk?

*It's usually what he does before going to bed.
He would stay awake for a full day
If he does not have a drink to put him to sleep.*

*It would be good
If the general knew about this.
Perhaps he doesn't see it, or his trusting
Sees only Cassio's virtues,
And not his evils. Doesn't that make sense?*

IAGO
[Aside to him] How now, Roderigo!
I pray you, after the lieutenant; go.
Exit RODERIGO

What is it, Roderigo!
Please, go after the lieutenant, now.

MONTANO
And 'tis great pity that the noble Moor
Should hazard such a place as his own second

With one of an ingraft infirmity:
It were an honest action to say
So to the Moor.

It's too bad that the good Moor
Should be so risky with his second-in-command by appointing
Someone with such a vice.
It would be honest to tell this
To the Moor.

IAGO
Not I, for this fair island:
I do love Cassio well; and would do much
To cure him of this evil--But, hark! what noise?

I won't tell him, not if you have me the whole island.
I love Cassio and would rather do what I can
To cure him instead of ruining him. But wait, what is that sound?

Cry within: 'Help! help!'
Re-enter CASSIO, driving in RODERIGO

CASSIO
You rogue! you rascal!

You villain and rascal!

MONTANO
What's the matter, lieutenant?

What is the matter, lieutenant?

CASSIO
A knave teach me my duty!
I'll beat the knave into a twiggen bottle.

You fool, trying to teach me my duty!
I will beat you until you are criss-crossed like a straw covered bottle.

RODERIGO
Beat me!

Beat me!?

CASSIO
Dost thou prate, rogue?
Striking RODERIGO

Are you talking, you villain?

MONTANO
Nay, good lieutenant;
Staying him
I pray you, sir, hold your hand.

Stop, good lieutenant.

Please, sir, hold yourself back.

CASSIO
Let me go, sir,
Or I'll knock you o'er the mazzard.

Let me go
Or I will knock on the head.

MONTANO
Come, come,
you're drunk.

Now, now, come on,
you are drunk.

CASSIO
Drunk!
They fight

Drunk!

IAGO
[Aside to RODERIGO]
Away, I say; go out, and cry a mutiny.
Exit RODERIGO
Nay, good lieutenant,--alas, gentlemen;--
Help, ho!--Lieutenant,--sir,--Montano,--sir;
Help, masters!--Here's a goodly watch indeed!

Bell rings
Who's that which rings the bell?--Diablo, ho!
The town will rise: God's will, lieutenant, hold!

You will be shamed for ever.
Re-enter OTHELLO and Attendants

Now go and cry out that there is a fight.

No, lieutenant, stop – oh, gentlemen –
Help! – Lieutenant – sir – Montano – sir –
Help, someone! – Fine way to guard the
night!

Who is ringing the bell? – Oh, damn!
The whole town will come out. By God,
lieutenant, stop!
You will be ruined forever.

OTHELLO
What is the matter here?

What is the matter here.

MONTANO
'Zounds, I bleed still; I am hurt to the death.
Faints

Oh I am bleeding! I am hurt to death.

OTHELLO
Hold, for your lives!

Stop, or your lives will be at stake!

IAGO
Hold, ho! Lieutenant,--sir--Montano,--gentlemen,--
Have you forgot all sense of place and duty?

Hold! the general speaks to you; hold, hold, for shame!

Stop! – Lieutenant – sir – Montano – men –
Have you all forgotten your sense of duty and
honor?
Stop! The general is speaking to you! Stop,
how shameful!

OTHELLO
Why, how now, ho! from whence ariseth this?
Are we turn'd Turks, and to ourselves do that
Which heaven hath forbid the Ottomites?

For Christian shame, put by this barbarous brawl:
He that stirs next to carve for his own rage
Holds his soul light; he dies upon his motion.

Silence that dreadful bell: it frights the isle
From her propriety. What is the matter, masters?
Honest Iago, that look'st dead with grieving,
Speak, who began this? on thy love, I charge thee.

Why, how! How did this happen?
Have we become the Turks ourselves, and thus
Do what heaven stopped the Turks from doing
to us?
For the sake of Christianity stop this fighting:
Whoever moves next to unleash his anger
Is risking his own life: he will die once he
moves.
Someone stop that awful bell, it is frightening
The islanders. What happened here, sirs?
Good Iago, you look exhausted and upset.
Speak up, who started this? I'm asking you
out of love.

IAGO
I do not know: friends all but now, even now,

I don't know. We were all friends until now,

In quarter, and in terms like bride and groom
Devesting them for bed; and then, but now--
As if some planet had unwitted men--

Swords out, and tilting one at other's breast,

In opposition bloody. I cannot speak
Any beginning to this peevish odds;
And would in action glorious I had lost
Those legs that brought me to a part of it!

OTHELLO
How comes it, Michael, you are thus forgot?

CASSIO
I pray you, pardon me; I cannot speak.

OTHELLO
Worthy Montano, you were wont be civil;
The gravity and stillness of your youth

The world hath noted, and your name is great

In mouths of wisest censure: what's the matter,
That you unlace your reputation thus
And spend your rich opinion for the name
Of a night-brawler? give me answer to it.

MONTANO
Worthy Othello, I am hurt to danger:
Your officer, Iago, can inform you,--
While I spare speech, which something now offends me,--
Of all that I do know: nor know I aught
By me that's said or done amiss this night;
Unless self-charity be sometimes a vice,
And to defend ourselves it be a sin
When violence assails us.

OTHELLO
Now, by heaven,
My blood begins my safer guides to rule;
And passion, having my best judgment collied,
Assays to lead the way: if I once stir,

Or do but lift this arm, the best of you
Shall sink in my rebuke. Give me to know
How this foul rout began, who set it on;
And he that is approved in this offence,
Though he had twinn'd with me, both at a birth,
Shall lose me. What! in a town of war,

We were like bride and groom
Undressing for bed, and then, just now –
As if the alignment of the planets had made
them crazy –
Swords came out, pointed at each other's
chest
In order to fight. I can't speak
To how this all began,
And I wish that in previous battles I had lost
My legs so I wouldn't have come to see this!

What happened, Michael, that you lost
yourself?

Please, forgive me. I cannot speak.

Worthy Montano, you have been so polite.
As a young man, your seriousness and
calmness
Was noted by the world, and your name is
mentioned
By the wisest men. What happened
That you ruin your reputation like this
And destroy these good estimations to become
Someone who fights at night? Give me an
answer.

Worthy Othello, I am badly injured.
Your officer, Iago, can tell you –
I should save my breath, it hurts me to talk –
He can tell you everything I know. I have done
Nothing wrong tonight,
Unless it is wrong to look out for ourselves
And a sin to defend ourselves
Against attack.

As God is my witness,
I am beginning to lose my temper.
Passion is dirtying my sound judgment
And wants to be in charge of my decision
making. If I move
Or lift this arm, everyone
Will suffer at my hands. Tell me
How this fighting started, and who began it.
Whoever is proved the offender,
Even if he were my twin at birth,
Shall lose my respect. Really! In a town
already avoiding a war,

Yet wild, the people's hearts brimful of fear,
To manage private and domestic quarrel,
In night, and on the court and guard of safety!

'Tis monstrous. Iago, who began't?

MONTANO
If partially affined, or leagued in office,

Thou dost deliver more or less than truth,
Thou art no soldier.

IAGO
Touch me not so near:
I had rather have this tongue cut from my mouth
Than it should do offence to Michael Cassio;
Yet, I persuade myself, to speak the truth
Shall nothing wrong him. Thus it is, general.

Montano and myself being in speech,
There comes a fellow crying out for help:
And Cassio following him with determined sword,
To execute upon him. Sir, this gentleman

Steps in to Cassio, and entreats his pause:
Myself the crying fellow did pursue,

Lest by his clamour--as it so fell out--
The town might fall in fright: he, swift of foot,

Outran my purpose; and I return'd the rather
For that I heard the clink and fall of swords,
And Cassio high in oath; which till to-night
I ne'er might say before. When I came back--
For this was brief--I found them close together,
At blow and thrust; even as again they were
When you yourself did part them.
More of this matter cannot I report:
But men are men; the best sometimes forget:

Though Cassio did some little wrong to him,
As men in rage strike those that wish them best,

Yet surely Cassio, I believe, received
From him that fled some strange indignity,
Which patience could not pass.

OTHELLO
I know, Iago,
Thy honesty and love doth mince this matter,

Where the people's hearts are already scared,
You have created this private fight
At night, when you were supposed to be on guard!
This is awful. Iago, who started it.

If you speak from partiality or are in league with the offender
And thus do not speak the real truth,
You are no soldier.

Do not say such things to me.
I would rather cut my tongue out of my mouth
Than speak ill of Michael Cassio.
Yes, I believe that by telling the truth
I do not do anything wrong to him. So here it is, general.
Montano and I were talking,
And a fellow came crying out for help.
Cassio was following him with a sword,
Intent on executing him. Sir, this gentelman Montano
Stepped in to stop Cassio,
And I followed after the man crying out for help,
So that his awful shouting
Would not terrify the town. He, being very fast,
Outran me, and I came back
Hearing the sound of swordfighting
And Cassio swearing, which until tonight
I have never heard before. When I returned –
This was quick – I found them together
Fighting, just as they were
When you separated them.
I have nothing more to say
Except that men are men, we forget this sometimes,
And though Cassio injured Montano,
Striking out of rage at whoever is close no matter who they are or their intentions are,
I am also certain that Cassio received
A cruel insult from the man who fled
Which even patience could not let pass.

I know, Iago,
That your honest and love affect your judgment

Making it light to Cassio. Cassio, I love thee

But never more be officer of mine.
Re-enter DESDEMONA, attended
Look, if my gentle love be not raised up!
I'll make thee an example.

DESDEMONA
What's the matter?

OTHELLO
All's well now, sweeting; come away to bed.
Sir, for your hurts, myself will be your surgeon:

Lead him off.
To MONTANO, who is led off
Iago, look with care about the town,
And silence those whom this vile brawl distracted.

Come, Desdemona: 'tis the soldiers' life
To have their balmy slumbers waked with strife.
Exeunt all but IAGO and CASSIO

IAGO
What, are you hurt, lieutenant?

CASSIO
Ay, past all surgery.

IAGO
Marry, heaven forbid!

CASSIO
Reputation, reputation, reputation! O, I have lost

my reputation! I have lost the immortal part of
myself, and what remains is bestial. My reputation,

Iago, my reputation!

IAGO
As I am an honest man, I thought you had received
some bodily wound; there is more sense in that than

in reputation. Reputation is an idle and most false

imposition: oft got without merit, and lost without

deserving: you have lost no reputation at all,
unless you repute yourself such a loser. What, man!

And seek to lighten Cassio's sin. Cassio, I love you,
But you are no longer my officer.

Look, you have woken my gentle love!
I will make an example out of you.

What happened?

All is well, sweetheart. Come back to bed.
Sir, for your injuries, I will make sure you are treated.
Lead him away.

Iago, go care for the townspeople
And calm them whom were woken by this fight.
Come Desdemona: it's the soldier's life
To have their sleep interrupted by fighting.

Are you hurt, lieutenant?

Yes, past all recovery.

No, I hope not!

Reputation, reputation, reputation! O, I have lose
my reputation! I have lost the eternal part of myself and only this animal side remains. My reputation,
Iago, my reputation!

I honestly thought that you had received
a physical injury – that means much more than
your reputation. Reputation is a lazy and fake quality
that others impose. Often it has no merit, and it can be lost without
warrant. You have lost no reputation unless you think you have. What!

there are ways to recover the general again: you

are but now cast in his mood, a punishment more in

policy than in malice, even so as one would beat his

offenceless dog to affright an imperious lion: sue
to him again, and he's yours.

CASSIO
I will rather sue to be despised than to deceive so
good a commander with so slight, so drunken, and so

indiscreet an officer. Drunk? and speak parrot?

and squabble? swagger? swear? and discourse
fustian with one's own shadow? O thou invisible
spirit of wine, if thou hast no name to be known by,
let us call thee devil!

IAGO
What was he that you followed with your sword? What
had he done to you?

CASSIO
I know not.

IAGO
Is't possible?

CASSIO
I remember a mass of things, but nothing distinctly;

a quarrel, but nothing wherefore. O God, that men

should put an enemy in their mouths to steal away

their brains! that we should, with joy, pleasance

revel and applause, transform ourselves into beasts!

IAGO
Why, but you are now well enough: how came

you thus recovered?

CASSIO
It hath pleased the devil drunkenness to give place

to the devil wrath; one unperfectness shows me

There are many ways to get back on the general's good side, right now
you are dealing with a mood of his, but the punishment came from
policy, not from ill-will, just as someone would beat
his dog to frighten off a lion. Go to him and ask, and he will change his mind.

I would rather ask him to hate me than to trick
a good commander to allow a worthless, drunken,
stupid officer back. Drunk? Speaking nonsense?
And swearing? Raving
At one's own shadow? O invisible
demon of wine, if you have no other name,
I will call you devil!

Who was he whom you were chasing with
your sword? What did he say to you?

I don't know.

Is that possible?

I remember a number of things, but nothing distinctly:
a fight, but nothing else. O God, how awful that men
would put an enemy into their mouths through wine that steals
their minds! How horrible that we should joyfully
party and thus transform ourselves into animals!

You seem very sober now, how did you recover so
quickly?

The devil called drunkenness went away and gave his spot
to the devil called wrath. One vice opens up to

another, to make me frankly despise myself.

IAGO
Come, you are too severe a moraler: as the time,
the place, and the condition of this country
stands, I could heartily wish this had not befallen;
but, since it is as it is, mend it for your own good.

CASSIO
I will ask him for my place again; he shall tell me
I am a drunkard! Had I as many mouths as Hydra,

such an answer would stop them all. To be now a
sensible man, by and by a fool, and presently a
beast! O strange! Every inordinate cup is
unblessed and the ingredient is a devil.

IAGO
Come, come, good wine is a good familiar
creature,
if it be well used: exclaim no more against it.
And, good lieutenant, I think you think I love you.

CASSIO
I have well approved it, sir. I drunk!

IAGO
You or any man living may be drunk! at a time,
man.
I'll tell you what you shall do. Our general's wife
is now the general: may say so in this respect, for
that he hath devoted and given up himself to the

contemplation, mark, and denotement of her parts
and
graces: confess yourself freely to her; importune
her help to put you in your place again: she is of
so free, so kind, so apt, so blessed a disposition,
she holds it a vice in her goodness not to do more
than she is requested: this broken joint between
you and her husband entreat her to splinter; and,
my fortunes against any lay worth naming, this
crack of your love shall grow stronger than it was
before.

CASSIO
You advise me well.

IAGO
I protest, in the sincerity of love and honest
kindness.

---

another, and makes me hate myself.

*You are much to hard on yourself. Given the time.
and your rank, and the condition of the island,
I of course wish this had not happened –
but since it has, try to work it for your own good.*

*If I ask him for my rank again he shall tell me
that I am an alcoholic! Even if I had as many mouths
as the Hydra of myth,
an answer like that would quiet them all. First I was a
reasonable person, and then I was a fool, and now I
am an animal! How strange! Every cup of wine
is an evil curse of the devil.*

Come now, wine is a good substance

*if it is used appropriately. Stop speaking against it,
And, good lieutenant, I think you know that I am your
friend.*

I know that well, sir. Me! A drunkard!

*You or any man might become drunk at any time,
my man.
This is what you shall now do: Othello's wife
is his general, which I say because
he has so devoted himself to her and given himself
away
to thinking about and noting her bodyparts and*

*qualities. Tell your story to her and beg
her to help you regain your rank. She is
so kind and has such a gracious nature
that she considers it wrongdoing to not help someone
as much as they ask. The brokenness between
you and Othello can be mended by her, and I
would bet that
the love between you two will grow to be even
stronger than it was before.*

You have good advice.

No, only the sincerity of my love and kindness for you.

CASSIO
I think it freely; and betimes in the morning I will
beseech the virtuous Desdemona to undertake for me:
I am desperate of my fortunes if they cheque me here.

*I believe you. Early tomorrow morning I will
go to good Desdemona and plead my case.
I am desperate to turn my fortunes around.*

IAGO
You are in the right. Good night, lieutenant;
I must to the watch.

*That's the right thing to do. Goodnight
lieutenant. I must go to keep the watch.*

CASSIO
Good night, honest Iago.
Exit

Goodnight, honest Iago.

IAGO
And what's he then that says I play the villain?
When this advice is free I give and honest,
Probal to thinking and indeed the course
To win the Moor again? For 'tis most easy

*And who says I am the villain?
My advice is so good and honest,
And it probably is the best course
To get back in the Moor's good favor. It is
very easy*

The inclining Desdemona to subdue
In any honest suit: she's framed as fruitful

*To convince the willing Desdemona to help
Any case since she has the best wishes for
others.*

As the free elements. And then for her
To win the Moor--were't to renounce his baptism,

*And then, for her
To convince the Moor – it could be as serious
as renouncing his baptism*

All seals and symbols of redeemed sin,
His soul is so enfetter'd to her love,
That she may make, unmake, do what she list,
Even as her appetite shall play the god

*And all the other marks of his salvation,
But he is so completely in love with her
That she can do whatever she wants
And through her desires have as much control
as God*

With his weak function. How am I then a villain

*Compared to his weak resistance. So how am
I a villain*

To counsel Cassio to this parallel course,
Directly to his good? Divinity of hell!

*To suggest to Cassio to take this course,
Which is for his benefit? I am like Satan
himself!*

When devils will the blackest sins put on,

*When devils are looking to do the most evil
sins they can,*

They do suggest at first with heavenly shows,
As I do now: for whiles this honest fool
Plies Desdemona to repair his fortunes
And she for him pleads strongly to the Moor,
I'll pour this pestilence into his ear,
That she repeals him for her body's lust;

*They first take on a heavenly appearance
Just as I am doing. While this honest fool
Seeks to get Desdemona to help him
And she pleads his case to the Moor,
I will poison his ear
With talk of her being disgusted at his
appearance*

And by how much she strives to do him good,
She shall undo her credit with the Moor.

*And so the stronger she strives to help Cassio,
The more she will become suspicious to the
Moor.*

So will I turn her virtue into pitch,
And out of her own goodness make the net
That shall enmesh them all.
Re-enter RODERIGO

*So I will turn her goodness into evil,
And out of it create a net
To trap them all.*

How now, Roderigo!

How are you, Roderigo?

RODERIGO
I do follow here in the chase, not like a hound that
hunts, but one that fills up the cry. My money is
almost spent; I have been to-night exceedingly well
cudgelled; and I think the issue will be, I shall
have so much experience for my pains, and so,
with no money at all and a little more wit, return
again to Venice.

*I am spent from the chase, not like the hound
hunting, but like the hunted. My money is
nearly gone and tonight I have been very brutally
beaten. I think that in return I have
gained more experience for my sufferings, so with
no money, and a little more wisdom, I am going
back to Venice.*

IAGO
How poor are they that have not patience!
What wound did ever heal but by degrees?
Thou know'st we work by wit, and not by
witchcraft;
And wit depends on dilatory time.
Does't not go well? Cassio hath beaten thee.
And thou, by that small hurt, hast cashier'd
Cassio:
Though other things grow fair against the sun,

Yet fruits that blossom first will first be ripe:
Content thyself awhile. By the mass, 'tis morning;
Pleasure and action make the hours seem short.
Retire thee; go where thou art billeted:
Away, I say; thou shalt know more hereafter:
Nay, get thee gone.
Exit RODERIGO
Two things are to be done:
My wife must move for Cassio to her mistress;
I'll set her on;
Myself the while to draw the Moor apart,
And bring him jump when he may Cassio find
Soliciting his wife: ay, that's the way
Dull not device by coldness and delay.

Exit

*How pathetic they are who do not have patience!
Don't wounds heal slowly, not all at once?
You know that we are working through trickery
not magic,
And such tricks require time.
Aren't you alright? Cassio beat you,
But because of that small injury, you have gotten
gotten Cassio discounted!
Our work is making the right things grow under the
sun,
And the fruits of this work will soon be ripe,
So be patient. My God, it's already morning:
Partying and action made time fly.
Go to sleep back where you are staying.
Go now, you will know more later.
No, get going.*

*Two things still must be done:
My wife must plead Cassio's case to Desdemona.
Which I can convince her to do.
Meanwhile I must go to the Moor
And make sure he sees Cassio
Pleading to his wife. Yes, thats what needs to happen,
And I must not ruin the plan through stupidity or
slowness.*

Act III

Scene I. Before the castle.

Enter CASSIO and some Musicians

CASSIO
Masters, play here; I will content your pains;
Something that's brief; and bid 'Good morrow,
general.'
Music
Enter Clown

Masters, play now – I will pay you.
Play something brief, but happy, and remember to say
"Good morning, general."

Clown
Why masters, have your instruments been in
Naples, that they speak i' the nose thus?

Why masters, have your instruments been to Naples?
Is that why they have a nasal sound?

First Musician
How, sir, how!

What!

Clown
Are these, I pray you, wind-instruments?

Please tell me, are these wind instruments?

First Musician
Ay, marry, are they, sir.

They are, sir, yes.

Clown
O, thereby hangs a tail.

There's the problem.

First Musician
Whereby hangs a tale, sir?

What is the problem, sir?

Clown
Marry, sir, by many a wind-instrument that I know.
But, masters, here's money for you: and the general
so likes your music, that he desires you, for love's
sake, to make no more noise with it.

Well, sir, I know many people who are all wind.
But, masters, here's some money. The general
likes your music so much that he desires, out of love,
that you stop making noise out of it.

First Musician
Well, sir, we will not.

Well then we will stop.

Clown
If you have any music that may not be heard, to't
again: but, as they say to hear music the general
does not greatly care.

If you have any music that makes no sound, do play it
again. But as I said, with music that can be heard, the
general does not care for that.

First Musician
We have none such, sir.

We have no music like that, sir.

Clown
Then put up your pipes in your bag, for I'll away:
go; vanish into air; away!

Then put your instruments away,
go, leave into the air, goodbye!

Exeunt Musicians

CASSIO
Dost thou hear, my honest friend?

Do you hear, my honest friend?

Clown
No, I hear not your honest friend; I hear you.

No, I don't hear your honest friend, but I hear you.

CASSIO
Prithee, keep up thy quillets. There's a poor piece

of gold for thee: if the gentlewoman that attends
the general's wife be stirring, tell her there's
one Cassio entreats her a little favour of speech:
wilt thou do this?

*Please, keep your jokes to yourself. Here's a bit
of money. If the woman who is attending to
the general's wife is up, tell her
Cassio would like to speak with her –
will you do this?*

Clown
She is stirring, sir: if she will stir hither, I
shall seem to notify unto her.

*She is up, sir, and if she comes this way, I
will tell her.*

CASSIO
Do, my good friend.
Exit Clown
Enter IAGO
In happy time, Iago.

Do, my friend.

Good to see you, Iago.

IAGO
You have not been a-bed, then?

Have you not slept yet?

CASSIO
Why, no; the day had broke
Before we parted. I have made bold, Iago,
To send in to your wife: my suit to her
Is, that she will to virtuous Desdemona

Procure me some access.

*No, the morning came
Before we parted. I decided, Iago,
To send after your wife and talk to her
In order to ask that she will go to virtuous
Desdemona
And find me access to talk to Desdemona.*

IAGO
I'll send her to you presently;
And I'll devise a mean to draw the Moor
Out of the way, that your converse and business
May be more free.

*I will send her to you now
And will devise a scheme to keep the Moor
Out of the way so that your conversation
Can be without interruption.*

CASSIO
I humbly thank you for't.
Exit IAGO
I never knew
A Florentine more kind and honest.
Enter EMILIA

Thank you.

*I never knew
A more kind and honest man from Florence.*

EMILIA
Good morrow, good Lieutenant: I am sorry
For your displeasure; but all will sure be well.

The general and his wife are talking of it;
And she speaks for you stoutly: the Moor replies,

That he you hurt is of great fame in Cyprus,
And great affinity, and that in wholesome wisdom

He might not but refuse you; but he protests he loves you
And needs no other suitor but his likings

To take the safest occasion by the front
To bring you in again.

CASSIO
Yet, I beseech you,
If you think fit, or that it may be done,
Give me advantage of some brief discourse
With Desdemona alone.

EMILIA
Pray you, come in;
I will bestow you where you shall have time
To speak your bosom freely.

CASSIO
I am much bound to you.
Exeunt

Good morning, good lieutenant. I am sorry
For your misfortunes, but I hope all will soon be fixed.
The general and his wife are talking about it
And she defends you very strongly. Then the Moor replies
That you hurt a very famous man in Cyprus,
One who is well liked, and that in the wisdom of the situation
He has no choice but to refuse you. Still, he says that he loves you
And that he needs no one to convince him, that by his own preference
He is looking for a safe time to
Reinstate you.

Still, I beg you,
If you think it is appropriate or possible,
Let me have some brief conversation
With Desdemona herself.

Yes, come in.
I will take you to where you will be able
To speak freely with her.

I am indebted to you.

Scene II. A room in the castle.

Enter OTHELLO, IAGO, and Gentlemen

OTHELLO
These letters give, Iago, to the pilot;
And by him do my duties to the senate:
That done, I will be walking on the works;

Repair there to me.

Iago, give these letters to the pilot
And ask him to pay my respects to the Senate.
With that done, I will be walking along the walls;
Find me there when you are done.

IAGO
Well, my good lord, I'll do't.

Very well, my lord. I will do it.

OTHELLO
This fortification, gentlemen, shall we see't?

Gentlemen, shall you show me around the fortifications?

Gentleman
We'll wait upon your lordship.
Exeunt

Whatever you would like, my lord.

Scene III. The garden of the castle.

Enter DESDEMONA, CASSIO, and EMILIA

DESDEMONA
Be thou assured, good Cassio, I will do
All my abilities in thy behalf.

Be certain, Cassio, that I will do
Everything I can.

EMILIA
Good madam, do: I warrant it grieves my husband,

As if the case were his.

Please do, madam. I believe it upsets my
husband so much
That it seems like it is his case.

DESDEMONA
O, that's an honest fellow. Do not doubt, Cassio,

But I will have my lord and you again

As friendly as you were.

O, well he is a good man. Do not doubt,
Cassio,
That I will make sure that you and my
husband
Become as friendly as you ever were.

CASSIO
Bounteous madam,
Whatever shall become of Michael Cassio,
He's never any thing but your true servant.

Good lady,
Whatever happens to me,
I will always be your devoted servant.

DESDEMONA
I know't; I thank you. You do love my lord:
You have known him long; and be you well assured

He shall in strangeness stand no further off
Than in a polite distance.

I know, thank you. You do love Othello,
And you have known him a long time. Be
assured:
He only stands away from you
From a political need.

CASSIO
Ay, but, lady,
That policy may either last so long,
Or feed upon such nice and waterish diet,

Or breed itself so out of circumstance,
That, I being absent and my place supplied,
My general will forget my love and service.

Yes, but lady,
That political need may go on for too long,
Or may create a such a diet and daily that I
am not missed,
Or may continue on unquestioned,
That, since I am gone and my position taken,
Othello will forget about my love and my
service to him.

DESDEMONA
Do not doubt that; before Emilia here

I give thee warrant of thy place: assure thee,
If I do vow a friendship, I'll perform it
To the last article: my lord shall never rest;
I'll watch him tame and talk him out of patience;

Do not think about that. Before Emilia as my
witness,
I promise you your position. Rest assured,
If I vow someone my friendship, I act on it
To my fullest. Othello shall never gain rest
Since I will watch him and talk to him until his
patience is gone,

His bed shall seem a school, his board a shrift;

I'll intermingle every thing he does
With Cassio's suit: therefore be merry, Cassio;
For thy solicitor shall rather die
Than give thy cause away.

EMILIA
Madam, here comes my lord.

CASSIO
Madam, I'll take my leave.

DESDEMONA
Why, stay, and hear me speak.

CASSIO
Madam, not now: I am very ill at ease,
Unfit for mine own purposes.

DESDEMONA
Well, do your discretion.
Exit CASSIO
Enter OTHELLO and IAGO

IAGO
Ha! I like not that.

OTHELLO
What dost thou say?

IAGO
Nothing, my lord: or if--I know not what.

OTHELLO
Was not that Cassio parted from my wife?

IAGO
Cassio, my lord! No, sure, I cannot think it,
That he would steal away so guilty-like,
Seeing you coming.

OTHELLO
I do believe 'twas he.

DESDEMONA
How now, my lord!
I have been talking with a suitor here,
A man that languishes in your displeasure.

*And his bed and dinner table will seem like a
school for all of my talking.
I will mix everything he does
With your case, so be happy, Cassio.
I, your attorney, would rather die
Than forget your cause.*

Madam, here comes Othello.

I will take my leave, madam.

No, stay, and hear what I will say.

*Madam, not now. I do not feel comfortable
And that will not help my case.*

As you will.

Well! I don't like that.

What is it?

Nothing, my lord – or it – I don't know.

Was that Cassio leaving my wife?

*Cassio! No, I don't think so.
He would not leave looking so guilty
From seeing you coming.*

I think it was him.

*Hello, my lord!
I have been talking with a man with a suit
Who suffers from your anger at him.*

OTHELLO
Who is't you mean?

Who are you talking about?

DESDEMONA
Why, your lieutenant, Cassio. Good my lord,
If I have any grace or power to move you,
His present reconciliation take;
For if he be not one that truly loves you,
That errs in ignorance and not in cunning,

I have no judgment in an honest face:
I prithee, call him back.

Why, Cassio, your lieutenant. Good lord,
If I have power to influence you,
Please accept his desire to reconcile.
He is someone who truly loves you
And his mistakes come from ignorance, not from
deviousness —
If I am wrong, I am an awful judge of character.
Please, call him back.

OTHELLO
Went he hence now?

Did he leave just now?

DESDEMONA
Ay, sooth; so humbled
That he hath left part of his grief with me,
To suffer with him. Good love, call him back.

Yes, he went away humbled
And left some of his sadness with me
So that I suffer with him. My love, call him back.

OTHELLO
Not now, sweet Desdemona; some other time.

Not yet, sweet Desdemona. Another time.

DESDEMONA
But shall't be shortly?

But will it be shortly?

OTHELLO
The sooner, sweet, for you.

Sooner than later, because you ask, sweetheart.

DESDEMONA
Shall't be to-night at supper?

Perhaps tonight at dinner?

OTHELLO
No, not to-night.

No, not tonight.

DESDEMONA
To-morrow dinner, then?

Tomorrow at dinner, then?

OTHELLO
I shall not dine at home;
I meet the captains at the citadel.

I will not be eating at home,
But meeting with the captains at the castle.

DESDEMONA
Why, then, to-morrow night; or Tuesday morn;
On Tuesday noon, or night; on Wednesday morn:

I prithee, name the time, but let it not
Exceed three days: in faith, he's penitent;
And yet his trespass, in our common reason--
Save that, they say, the wars must make examples

Then tomorrow night, or Tuesday morning,
Or Tuesday at noon, or night, or on Wednesday
morning,
But please name the time, and do not let it
Go past three days because, truly, he is remorseful.
And anyway, his offense, in all reason —
Though, of course in wartime examples must be made

Out of their best--is not almost a fault
To incur a private cheque. When shall he come?

Tell me, Othello: I wonder in my soul,
What you would ask me, that I should deny,

Or stand so mammering on. What! Michael Cassio,

That came a-wooing with you, and so many a time,

When I have spoke of you dispraisingly,
Hath ta'en your part; to have so much to do

To bring him in! Trust me, I could do much,--

OTHELLO
Prithee, no more: let him come when he will;

I will deny thee nothing.

DESDEMONA
Why, this is not a boon;
'Tis as I should entreat you wear your gloves,

Or feed on nourishing dishes, or keep you warm,
Or sue to you to do a peculiar profit
To your own person: nay, when I have a suit
Wherein I mean to touch your love indeed,
It shall be full of poise and difficult weight
And fearful to be granted.

OTHELLO
I will deny thee nothing:
Whereon, I do beseech thee, grant me this,
To leave me but a little to myself.

DESDEMONA
Shall I deny you? no: farewell, my lord.

OTHELLO
Farewell, my Desdemona: I'll come to thee straight.

DESDEMONA
Emilia, come. Be as your fancies teach you;
Whate'er you be, I am obedient.
Exeunt DESDEMONA and EMILIA

OTHELLO
Excellent wretch! Perdition catch my soul,
But I do love thee! and when I love thee not,

Out of the best of men – is not a fault
So great that it deserves such punishment.
When should he come?
Tell me, Othello. I wonder:
Is there anything you could ask me that I
would deny you
Or stand muttering about? This is Michael
Cassio,
He who came with you to woo me so many
times,
Who, when I criticized you to him,
Took your side and defended you, and now I
have to make so much noise
just so you will bring him back! Trust me, I
can do much more –

Please, no more. He can come back when he
wants,
I will deny you nothing.

It's not like you are doing me a favor:
It's just like if I were to tell you to wear gloves
in the cold
Or eat healthy food, or stay warm
Or request you to do anything that will profit
yourself. No, when I have a request
Where I need to appeal to your love for me,
It will be one that is very difficult
And terrible to be granted.

I will deny you nothing,
But please, grant me one thing:
Leave me a lone for a little while.

Would I deny you? No. Goodbye, my lord.

Goodbye, my Desdemona. I will come to you
soon.

Emilia, come. Othello, do what you feel like,
Whatever you do, I will obey you.

Wonderful woman! Heaven help me,
But I love you! And if I stop loving you,

Chaos is come again.

May the universe return to Chaos, as it was before the world was made.

IAGO
My noble lord--

My noble lord–

OTHELLO
What dost thou say, Iago?

What is it, Iago?

IAGO
Did Michael Cassio, when you woo'd my lady,
Know of your love?

*Did Michael Cassio, when you courted Desdemona,
Know about your love for her?*

OTHELLO
He did, from first to last: why dost thou ask?

He did, right from the beginning, why?

IAGO
But for a satisfaction of my thought;
No further harm.

*Just for my own curiosity,
No other reason.*

OTHELLO
Why of thy thought, Iago?

What are you curious about, Iago?

IAGO
I did not think he had been acquainted with her.

I did not know that he knew her.

OTHELLO
O, yes; and went between us very oft.

O yes, and he talked to her for me often.

IAGO
Indeed!

Really!

OTHELLO
Indeed! ay, indeed: discern'st thou aught in that?
Is he not honest?

*Yes, really: is there something wrong with that?
Don't you think he is honest?*

IAGO
Honest, my lord!

Honest, my lord!

OTHELLO
Honest! ay, honest.

Honest! yes, honest.

IAGO
My lord, for aught I know.

For all I know, my lord.

OTHELLO
What dost thou think?

And what do you think?

IAGO
Think, my lord!

What do I think, my lord?

OTHELLO
Think, my lord!
By heaven, he echoes me,
As if there were some monster in his thought
Too hideous to be shown. Thou dost mean something:

I heard thee say even now, thou likedst not that,
When Cassio left my wife: what didst not like?

And when I told thee he was of my counsel
In my whole course of wooing, thou criedst 'Indeed!'

And didst contract and purse thy brow together,
As if thou then hadst shut up in thy brain
Some horrible conceit: if thou dost love me,
Show me thy thought.

IAGO
My lord, you know I love you.

OTHELLO
I think thou dost;
And, for I know thou'rt full of love and honesty,
And weigh'st thy words before thou givest them breath,

Therefore these stops of thine fright me the more:
For such things in a false disloyal knave
Are tricks of custom, but in a man that's just

They are close delations, working from the heart
That passion cannot rule.

IAGO
 For Michael Cassio,
I dare be sworn I think that he is honest.

OTHELLO
I think so too.

IAGO
Men should be what they seem;
Or those that be not, would they might seem none!

OTHELLO
Certain, men should be what they seem.

IAGO
Why, then, I think Cassio's an honest man.

OTHELLO
Nay, yet there's more in this:

What do I think, my lord?
By God, he repeats what I say
As if he is thinking something so monstrous
That he must hide hit. You must mean
something that you won't tell me:
I heard you comment as if you did not like it
When you saw Cassio leave my wife. Why did
you not like it?
And when I told you he helped me
When I was courting Desdemona you cried
out, "Really!"
While you wrinkled your brow
As if you had thought of some
Awful imagination. If you love me,
Tell me what you thought.

My lord, you know I love you.

I think you do,
And I know that you are loving and honest,
That you weigh your words carefully before
you speak,
So your pauses even more frighten me.
In a disloyal liar,
These are common tricks, but in a man who is
just
They are indictments that work in the heart
And even passion cannot stop them.

As for Michael Cassio,
I swear that I think he is honest.

I agree.

Men should be what they look like they are,
And those that are not honest should not seem
honest!

Agreed, men should be in reality what they
look like they are.

Then I think Cassio is in reality an honest
man.

No, there's more to it than this.

I prithee, speak to me as to thy thinkings,
As thou dost ruminate, and give thy worst of thoughts

The worst of words.

IAGO
Good my lord, pardon me:
Though I am bound to every act of duty,
I am not bound to that all slaves are free to.

Utter my thoughts? Why, say they are vile and false;

As where's that palace whereinto foul things
Sometimes intrude not? who has a breast so pure,

But some uncleanly apprehensions
Keep leets and law-days and in session sit
With meditations lawful?

OTHELLO
Thou dost conspire against thy friend, Iago,

If thou but think'st him wrong'd and makest his ear

A stranger to thy thoughts.

IAGO
I do beseech you--
Though I perchance am vicious in my guess,
As, I confess, it is my nature's plague
To spy into abuses, and oft my jealousy

Shapes faults that are not--that your wisdom yet,

From one that so imperfectly conceits,
Would take no notice, nor build yourself a trouble
Out of his scattering and unsure observance.

It were not for your quiet nor your good,
Nor for my manhood, honesty, or wisdom,

To let you know my thoughts.

OTHELLO
What dost thou mean?

IAGO
Good name in man and woman, dear my lord,
Is the immediate jewel of their souls:
Who steals my purse steals trash; 'tis something,
nothing;

Please, tell me what you are thinking,
Whatever you are pondering, and say even
your worst fears
Clearly, in their awful content.

My lord, please excuse me:
Though I will obey everything you ask,
I do not need to obey that which even slaves
are not forced to do.
Tell you my thoughts? What if they are awful
and wrong,
Since there is no place where awful things
Might enter into, and similarly no one has a
mind so pure
That no unclean, dirty thoughts
Sometimes come into it and mingle
With their pure thoughts and meditaitons.

You are working against your own friend,
Iago,
If you think he has been wronged and yet keep
him
Away from your thoughts.

I beg you –
Since I am often too suspicious
And, truly, it is a curse of my character
That I imagine problems and often my
imaginations
Create faults where there are none – that your
mind,
From someone who inaccurately imagines,
Will not be troubled by me or
What I have uncertainly and haphazardly
observed.
It would harm your peace and your goodness,
And I would sooner give up my manhood,
honesty, or intelligence
Than tell you what I think.

What do you mean?

A man and a woman's reputation, my lord,
Is the most worthy part of who they are:
If someone steals my money, they steal trash.
It is something, and then nothing,

'Twas mine, 'tis his, and has been slave to thousands:

But he that filches from me my good name
Robs me of that which not enriches him
And makes me poor indeed.

OTHELLO
By heaven, I'll know thy thoughts.

IAGO
You cannot, if my heart were in your hand;

Nor shall not, whilst 'tis in my custody.

OTHELLO
Ha!

IAGO
O, beware, my lord, of jealousy;
It is the green-eyed monster which doth mock
The meat it feeds on; that cuckold lives in bliss
Who, certain of his fate, loves not his wronger;

But, O, what damned minutes tells he o'er
Who dotes, yet doubts, suspects, yet strongly loves!

OTHELLO
O misery!

IAGO
Poor and content is rich and rich enough,
But riches fineless is as poor as winter

To him that ever fears he shall be poor.
Good heaven, the souls of all my tribe defend
From jealousy!

OTHELLO
Why, why is this?
Think'st thou I'ld make a lie of jealousy,
To follow still the changes of the moon

With fresh suspicions? No; to be once in doubt

Is once to be resolved: exchange me for a goat,

When I shall turn the business of my soul
To such exsufflicate and blown surmises,
Matching thy inference. 'Tis not to make me jealous

It was mine and now it is his, and it has been owned by thousands before.
But whoever steals my reputation
Takes away something that does not help him
But all the while truly hurts me.

By God, tell me what you think.

You cannot know, not even if you held my heart,
Which you can't since it is still in my body.

Ha!

My lord, be careful not to fall into jealousy.
It is a green eyed monster who taunts
Its victim. The man who is cheated on is happy
If he knows he is being cheated on and does not love the other man.
But O how horrible for the man
Who loves, yet doubts his beloved and is suspicious, yet still loves!

What misery!

Being poor and happy is rich enough,
But he who is rich without measure is as poor as winter is
If he fears that he will someday be poor.
Dear God, protect all of us
For jealousy!

Why do you say all of this?
Do you think that I will become so jealous
That I will watch for the moon to change phases
And get suspicious each time it does? No, if I became doubtful,
I would then become resolved to end doubt. I would sooner be a goat
Than spend my energy on
Such meaningless and trivial guesswork,
Looking to infer what has happened. It will not make me jealous

To say my wife is fair, feeds well, loves company,

Is free of speech, sings, plays and dances well;

Where virtue is, these are more virtuous:
Nor from mine own weak merits will I draw

The smallest fear or doubt of her revolt;
For she had eyes, and chose me. No, Iago;

I'll see before I doubt; when I doubt, prove;

And on the proof, there is no more but this,--
Away at once with love or jealousy!

IAGO
I am glad of it; for now I shall have reason
To show the love and duty that I bear you
With franker spirit: therefore, as I am bound,

Receive it from me. I speak not yet of proof.
Look to your wife; observe her well with Cassio;

Wear your eye thus, not jealous nor secure:

I would not have your free and noble nature,

Out of self-bounty, be abused; look to't:

I know our country disposition well;
In Venice they do let heaven see the pranks
They dare not show their husbands; their best conscience

Is not to leave't undone, but keep't unknown.

OTHELLO
Dost thou say so?

IAGO
She did deceive her father, marrying you;

And when she seem'd to shake and fear your looks,
She loved them most.

OTHELLO
And so she did.

IAGO
Why, go to then;
She that, so young, could give out such a seeming,
To seal her father's eyes up close as oak-

---

*To hear that my wife is beautiful, cooks well,
enjoys company,
Speaks freely, sings and has fun and dances
well –
These are only great things, and she is great.
I will not overcompensate for my weakness by
creating
A fear or doubt of her leaving me.
She had eyes and was not tricked, and she still
chose me. No, Iago,
I would look before I begin to doubt, and then
if I were to doubt, I would find proof,
And as for proof, there is nothing –
So my love will do away with jealousy!*

*I am glad, because now I have reason
To love you and obey your requests
With a more honest spirit. Therefore, since
you have asked,
I will tell you. I do not have proof of anything.
Look at your wife, and look at her when she is
with Cassio.
Behave like this, carefully, but neither jealous
nor unaware.
I would not want your noble and trusting
character
From someone else's gain, be taken
advantage of. So be wary.
I know the people of our county well –
In Venice, they let God see their sins,
But they never show these sins to their
husbands. They think it is best
When they can sin, but keep it unknown to
everyone.*

Do you really think so?

*She already tricked her father by marrying
you,
And she acted scared about your appearance
Even though she loved it most.*

Yes, she did.

*Well, there it is:
She who was so young put on such an act
To trick her father*

He thought 'twas witchcraft--but I am much to blame;

I humbly do beseech you of your pardon
For too much loving you.

OTHELLO
I am bound to thee for ever.

IAGO
I see this hath a little dash'd your spirits.

OTHELLO
Not a jot, not a jot.

IAGO
I' faith, I fear it has.
I hope you will consider what is spoke
Comes from my love. But I do see you're moved:
I am to pray you not to strain my speech

To grosser issues nor to larger reach

Than to suspicion.

OTHELLO
I will not.

IAGO
Should you do so, my lord,
My speech should fall into such vile success
As my thoughts aim not at. Cassio's my worthy friend--
My lord, I see you're moved.

OTHELLO
No, not much moved:
I do not think but Desdemona's honest.

IAGO
Long live she so! and long live you to think so!

OTHELLO
And yet, how nature erring from itself,--

IAGO
Ay, there's the point: as--to be bold with you--
Not to affect many proposed matches
Of her own clime, complexion, and degree,

Whereto we see in all things nature tends--
Foh! one may smell in such a will most rank,

That he thought it was witchcraft – but I shouldn't say that.
I ask for your forgiveness for speaking
Which I do only because I love you too much.

I owe you forever.

I see this has upset you a little.

Not at all, not at all.

Truly, I am afraid it has.
I hope that you know that what I said
Came from love. But I see that you are sad.
Please do not take what I have said so seriously
That you stretch it to greater imaginations and situations
Than the appropriate suspicion it deserves.

I will not.

If you do, my lord,
Then what I have said has had awful effects
That I did not intend. Cassio is a good friend-
My lord, I see that you are upset.

No, not that upset.
I think that Desdemona is very honest.

And may she be her whole life! And may your whole life you think so!

And yet, one can act against one's true nature-

Ah, that is what I meant. To be bold,
She was not affected by any proposals
From men who are more similar to her, as in country, skin color, and status,
Which nature tends to respect most –
Oh! One can almost sense such a disgusting will

Foul disproportion thoughts unnatural.
But pardon me; I do not in position
Distinctly speak of her; though I may fear
Her will, recoiling to her better judgment,
May fall to match you with her country forms
And happily repent.

In evilly overestimating such unnatural things!
But excuse me, I don't mean
To speak specifically of her. Though, still, I worry
That her desires, against her better judgement,
Will compare you to her countrymen
And choose them instead.

OTHELLO
Farewell, farewell:
If more thou dost perceive, let me know more;
Set on thy wife to observe: leave me, Iago:

Goodbye, goodbye –
If you see more, let me know,
And ask your wife to watch her. Go now, Iago.

IAGO
[Going] My lord, I take my leave.

My lord, I will go now.

OTHELLO
Why did I marry? This honest creature doubtless
Sees and knows more, much more, than he
unfolds.

Why did I even marry? This honest man must
See and know much more than he says.

IAGO
[Returning]
My lord, I would I might entreat your honour
To scan this thing no further; leave it to time:
Though it be fit that Cassio have his place,
For sure, he fills it up with great ability,
Yet, if you please to hold him off awhile,
You shall by that perceive him and his means:
Note, if your lady strain his entertainment
With any strong or vehement importunity;
Much will be seen in that. In the mean time,
Let me be thought too busy in my fears--
As worthy cause I have to fear I am--
And hold her free, I do beseech your honour.

My lord, I must ask you
To stop thinking about this thing. Give it time.
Though it is right that Cassio get his rank back,
After all he is very able and talented,
But if you hold him from accepting him for a while
You will see how he handles it.
If your lady continues to insist on his return
By strongly begging you –
You will see a lot in that. Meanwhile,
Think of me as too paranoid –
For I often am –
And hold her as blameless, please.

OTHELLO
Fear not my government.

Do not worry about my judgment.

IAGO
I once more take my leave.
Exit

Again, I will go now.

OTHELLO
This fellow's of exceeding honesty,
And knows all qualities, with a learned spirit,
Of human dealings. If I do prove her haggard,

Iago is incredibly honest
And speaks wisely of the qualities
Of other men. If I do find out she has been cheating
on me,

Though that her jesses were my dear heartstrings,
I'ld whistle her off and let her down the wind,
To pray at fortune. Haply, for I am black
And have not those soft parts of conversation

Even though she is tied to my very heartstrings
I will send her off
To her own luck. Maybe because I am black
And do not have the skilled softness of speech

That chamberers have, or for I am declined

Into the vale of years,--yet that's not much--
She's gone. I am abused; and my relief

Must be to loathe her. O curse of marriage,
That we can call these delicate creatures ours,
And not their appetites! I had rather be a toad,

And live upon the vapour of a dungeon,

Than keep a corner in the thing I love
For others' uses. Yet, 'tis the plague of great ones;

Prerogatived are they less than the base;
'Tis destiny unshunnable, like death:
Even then this forked plague is fated to us
When we do quicken. Desdemona comes:
Re-enter DESDEMONA and EMILIA
If she be false, O, then heaven mocks itself!
I'll not believe't.

DESDEMONA
How now, my dear Othello!
Your dinner, and the generous islanders

By you invited, do attend your presence.

OTHELLO
I am to blame.

DESDEMONA
Why do you speak so faintly?
Are you not well?

OTHELLO
I have a pain upon my forehead here.

DESDEMONA
'Faith, that's with watching; 'twill away again:

Let me but bind it hard, within this hour
It will be well.

OTHELLO
Your napkin is too little:
He puts the handkerchief from him; and it drops
Let it alone. Come, I'll go in with you.

DESDEMONA
I am very sorry that you are not well.

That mannered men have, or because I have aged
And am now old – yet not too old –
She leaves me. I have been wronged and my only hope
Is to hate her. Marriage is such a curse:
We think we can own these beautiful women,
And yet we cannot own their desires! I would rather be a frog
Living on the germ-ridden air and mold of a dungeon
Than to have only part of the woman I love
And share her with others. This is the pague of great men:
They are less favored than lower men,
It's an unshakeable destiny, like death.
We are fated to walk down this plagued path
From our birth. Here is Desdemona.

If she has lied, then God is mocking himself!
I will not believe it.

How are you, dear Othello!
Your dinner is waiting for you, and the islanders
Whom you invited want to see you at dinner.

It is my fault.

Why do you speak so quietly?
Are you sick?

I have a headache.

That's from the guard and not sleeping. It will go away.
Let me wrap it tightly and in an hour
It will be alright.

This is a little too tight.

Leave it alone. Come on, I will go with you.

I am sorry that you are not feeling well.

Exeunt OTHELLO and DESDEMONA

EMILIA
I am glad I have found this napkin:
This was her first remembrance from the Moor:
My wayward husband hath a hundred times
Woo'd me to steal it; but she so loves the token,
For he conjured her she should ever keep it,
That she reserves it evermore about her
To kiss and talk to. I'll have the work ta'en out,

And give't Iago: what he will do with it
Heaven knows, not I;
I nothing but to please his fantasy.
Re-enter Iago

I am glad I found this napkin –
It is her first keepsake from the Moor.
My evil husband has asked me a hundred times
To steal it from her, but she loves it,
Since Othello asked her to keep it,
So she keeps it near her
In order to talk to it and kiss it. I will have the pattern copied
And given to Iago. What he does with it
Heaven knows, but I don't.
I do whatever I can to please him.

IAGO
How now! what do you here alone?

What's going on? Why are you here alone?

EMILIA
Do not you chide; I have a thing for you.

Do not be mean to me. I have something for you.

IAGO
A thing for me? it is a common thing--

Something for me? Well you give that to everyone...

EMILIA
Ha!

Ha!

IAGO
To have a foolish wife.

O, to have a dumb wife.

EMILIA
O, is that all? What will you give me now
For the same handkerchief?

Are you done? What will you give me
In exchange for the handkerchief?

IAGO
What handkerchief?

What handkerchief?

EMILIA
What handkerchief?
Why, that the Moor first gave to Desdemona;
That which so often you did bid me steal.

What handkerchief?
The same one that the Moor gave to Desdemona
Which you have wanted me to steal.

IAGO
Hast stol'n it from her?

And you stole it?

EMILIA
No, 'faith; she let it drop by negligence.
And, to the advantage, I, being here, took't up.
Look, here it is.

No, of course not. She let it drop in passing
And, fortunately, I was here, and picked it up.
Here it is.

IAGO
A good wench; give it me.

You are a good woman. Give it to me.

EMILIA
What will you do with 't, that you have been so earnest
To have me filch it?

What will you do with it? Why were you so
Intent. On me taking it?

IAGO
[Snatching it] Why, what's that to you?

How is that your business?

EMILIA
If it be not for some purpose of import,
Give't me again: poor lady, she'll run mad
When she shall lack it.

If it is not for some important business
Then give it back. The poor lady will go mad
When she sees she does not have it.

IAGO
Be not acknown on 't; I have use for it.

Go, leave me.
Exit EMILIA
I will in Cassio's lodging lose this napkin,
And let him find it. Trifles light as air
Are to the jealous confirmations strong

As proofs of holy writ: this may do something.
The Moor already changes with my poison:

Dangerous conceits are, in their natures, poisons.
Which at the first are scarce found to distaste,
But with a little act upon the blood.
Burn like the mines of Sulphur. I did say so:
Look, where he comes!
Re-enter OTHELLO
Not poppy, nor mandragora,
Nor all the drowsy syrups of the world,
Shall ever medicine thee to that sweet sleep
Which thou owedst yesterday.

Do not admit you know where it is. I need it
for a reason.
Go, leave me.

I will place this napkin in Cassio's place
And make sure he finds it. Such a little thing
Becomes the confirmation of a jealous man's
thoughts,
As if they were holy proof. This might work.
The Moor is already affected by what I said to
him.
Evil ideas are really just like poisons:
At first, they aren't even distasted,
But then they get into the blood.
There they burn like mines of sulphur.
Look, here he comes!

No flower
Or medicine in all the world
Will ever force you into the sweet sleep
That you had yesterday.

OTHELLO
Ha! ha! false to me?

Ah! Is she cheating on me?

IAGO
Why, how now, general! no more of that.

What? Now, general, no more of that!

OTHELLO
Avaunt! be gone! thou hast set me on the rack:

I swear 'tis better to be much abused

Than but to know't a little.

Go away! You have place me on the torture
rack.
It is better to be taken advantage of
completely
Than to know about it at all.

IAGO
How now, my lord!

What are you saying, my lord!

OTHELLO
What sense had I of her stol'n hours of lust?

Did I know anything of the hours she spent cheating on me?

I saw't not, thought it not, it harm'd not me:
I slept the next night well, was free and merry;
I found not Cassio's kisses on her lips:
He that is robb'd, not wanting what is stol'n,
Let him not know't, and he's not robb'd at all.

I didn't see it or think it, and it didn't hurt me.
I slept well, and was happy.
I never tasted Cassio on her lips.
Whoever is robbed but does not notice it
Should never be told, since he is not really robbed at all.

IAGO
I am sorry to hear this.

I am sorry to hear this.

OTHELLO
I had been happy, if the general camp,

I would have been happier if the entire squadron,

Pioners and all, had tasted her sweet body,

Even the lowest ranking soldiers, had had sex with her,

So I had nothing known. O, now, for ever
Farewell the tranquil mind! farewell content!
Farewell the plumed troop, and the big wars,
That make ambition virtue! O, farewell!
Farewell the neighing steed, and the shrill trump,

As long as I didn't know. And now, forever,
Goodbye peaceful mind! Goodbye happiness!
Goodbye to the soldiers and wars
That make one great! O, goodbye!
Goodbye to the neighing horse and loud trumpet,

The spirit-stirring drum, the ear-piercing fife,
The royal banner, and all quality,
Pride, pomp and circumstance of glorious war!
And, O you mortal engines, whose rude throats
The immortal Jove's dead clamours counterfeit,
Farewell! Othello's occupation's gone!

The patriotic drum, the flute,
The royal flag and all the glory,
The pride, festivity, and situations of war!
And you, the cannons whose sounds
Rival Jove's thunderbolts,
Goodbye! My career is ruined!

IAGO
Is't possible, my lord?

Is that possible, my lord?

OTHELLO
Villain, be sure thou prove my love a whore,

Villain, you had better be sure that you can prove my love is a whore.

Be sure of it; give me the ocular proof:
Or by the worth of man's eternal soul
Thou hadst been better have been born a dog
Than answer my waked wrath!

Be sure of it and give me visible proof,
Or I swear by a man's eternal soul
That you would rather have been born a dog
Than stand in front of my anger!

IAGO
Is't come to this?

Has it come to this?

OTHELLO
Make me to see't; or, at the least, so prove it,
That the probation bear no hinge nor loop

Make me see it, or at the least, prove it
So that there is no possible explanation

To hang a doubt on; or woe upon thy life!

IAGO
My noble lord,--

OTHELLO
If thou dost slander her and torture me,

Never pray more; abandon all remorse;

On horror's head horrors accumulate;
Do deeds to make heaven weep, all earth amazed;

For nothing canst thou to damnation add
Greater than that.

IAGO
O grace! O heaven forgive me!
Are you a man? have you a soul or sense?

God be wi' you; take mine office. O wretched fool.
That livest to make thine honesty a vice!

O monstrous world! Take note, take note, O world,
To be direct and honest is not safe.
I thank you for this profit; and from hence

I'll love no friend, sith love breeds such offence.

OTHELLO
Nay, stay: thou shouldst be honest.

IAGO
I should be wise, for honesty's a fool
And loses that it works for.

OTHELLO
By the world,
I think my wife be honest and think she is not;
I think that thou art just and think thou art not.

I'll have some proof. Her name, that was as fresh
As Dian's visage, is now begrimed and black

As mine own face. If there be cords, or knives,

Poison, or fire, or suffocating streams,
I'll not endure it. Would I were satisfied!

That doubts it, or your life will be destroyed!

My noble lord –

If you are speaking poorly of her in order to torture me,
Then you should stop praying. Do not think you can repent.
On your head evil deeds will be numbered,
So do such awful things that heaven cries and all of the earth is stunned.
Nothing can add to the damnation
You would already receive.

O God! O God forgive me!
Are you still a man, and do you still have sense?
Please, I resign my rank. I am a fool,
For living to tell the truth and then seeing that it is a vice!
O awful world! O world, be forewarned:
It is not safe to be honest and straightforward.
Thank you for teaching me this, and from now on
I will give such love to no one, since it only hurts them.

No, stay, you should be honest.

No, I should be wise. Honesty is foolish
And loses the friendship it works to serve.

By God,
I think my wife is honest and dishonest,
And that you are trustworthy and untrustworthy.
I need proof. Her name, that was as pure
As the Goddess Diana, is now tainted and as black
As my face. As long as there are ropes or knives
Or poison or fire or streams to drown in,
I won't stand for this. I wish I knew the truth!

IAGO
I see, sir, you are eaten up with passion:
I do repent me that I put it to you.
You would be satisfied?

Sir, you are consumed by passion and strong feeling,
And I feel sorry that I did this.
You really want to know?

OTHELLO
Would! nay, I will.

Want! No, I will know.

IAGO
And may: but, how? how satisfied, my lord?

Would you, the supervisor, grossly gape on--
Behold her topp'd?

And you might, but how? How will you know, my lord?
Will you try to hide and watch –
Watch her have sex?

OTHELLO
Death and damnation! O!

Curses!

IAGO
It were a tedious difficulty, I think,
To bring them to that prospect: damn them then,
If ever mortal eyes do see them bolster
More than their own! What then? how then?
What shall I say? Where's satisfaction?
It is impossible you should see this,
Were they as prime as goats, as hot as monkeys,

It seems like it would be very difficult
To make sure you do that. Damn them
If anyone else's eyes see them
Do what they shouldn't be! So what can we do?
What can I say, how can you find proof?
It seems impossible that you will see them having sex,
Even if they were as ready as goats or as hot as monkeys,

As salt as wolves in pride, and fools as gross
As ignorance made drunk. But yet, I say,
If imputation and strong circumstances,
Which lead directly to the door of truth,
Will give you satisfaction, you may have't.

As horny as wolves, and as foolish as
Drunken morons. But, I wonder,
If calculations and circumstantial evidence,
Which in inference lead towards the truth,
Might give you the proof you need, you would accept it.

OTHELLO
Give me a living reason she's disloyal.

Give me a good reason that she is disloyal to me.

IAGO
I do not like the office:
But, sith I am enter'd in this cause so far,
Prick'd to't by foolish honesty and love,
I will go on. I lay with Cassio lately;
And, being troubled with a raging tooth,
I could not sleep.
There are a kind of men so loose of soul,
That in their sleeps will mutter their affairs:
One of this kind is Cassio:
In sleep I heard him say 'Sweet Desdemona,

I do not like this task,
But, since I am already this far in,
Led to it by foolish honesty and my love for you,
I will continue. I slept near Cassio lately
And, in pain from a toothache,
I could not sleep.
Some men have a loose soul
That causes them to talk in their sleep –
Cassio is a man like that.
While he was asleep I heard him say, "Sweet Desdemona,

Let us be wary, let us hide our loves;'
And then, sir, would he gripe and wring my hand
Cry 'O sweet creature!' and then kiss me hard,
As if he pluck'd up kisses by the roots

Let us be careful and hide our love"
And then, sir, he grabbed and held onto my hand
Crying "Sweet darling!" and then kissing me hard
As if he were taking the kisses out by force

That grew upon my lips: then laid his leg
Over my thigh, and sigh'd, and kiss'd; and then

Cried 'Cursed fate that gave thee to the Moor!'

OTHELLO
O monstrous! monstrous!

IAGO
Nay, this was but his dream.

OTHELLO
But this denoted a foregone conclusion:

'Tis a shrewd doubt, though it be but a dream.

IAGO
And this may help to thicken other proofs
That do demonstrate thinly.

OTHELLO
I'll tear her all to pieces.

IAGO
Nay, but be wise: yet we see nothing done;
She may be honest yet. Tell me but this,
Have you not sometimes seen a handkerchief
Spotted with strawberries in your wife's hand?

OTHELLO
I gave her such a one; 'twas my first gift.

IAGO
I know not that; but such a handkerchief--

I am sure it was your wife's--did I to-day
See Cassio wipe his beard with.

OTHELLO
If it be that--

IAGO
If it be that, or any that was hers,

It speaks against her with the other proofs.

OTHELLO
O, that the slave had forty thousand lives!
One is too poor, too weak for my revenge.
Now do I see 'tis true. Look here, Iago;

From my lips. Then he placed his leg
Over my thigh, and sighed, and kisse me
again,
And cried out "How awful that you belong to
the Moor!"

O awful! awful!

No, this was only a dream.

But it marks something that already
happened.
It's a good reason to doubt, even though it is
only a dream.

It may help support other proofs,
If they are not very convincing on their own.

I will destroy her!

No, be smart. We do not know anything yet,
She might be honest. Tell me this:
Have you seen a handkerchief
Spotted with strawberries, held by your wife?

I gave it to her, it was my first gift to her.

I did not know about that, but this
handkerchief –
I am sure it was your wife's – I saw today,
And Cassio wiped his beard with it.

If that was hers–

If it was hers, or anything else that belonged
to her,
Then it speaks strongly against her alongside
the other proofs.

O, if Cassio had forty thousand lives!
One life is too few for me to get my revenge.
Now I see it is true. Look, Iago,

All my fond love thus do I blow to heaven.
'Tis gone.
Arise, black vengeance, from thy hollow cell!
Yield up, O love, thy crown and hearted throne
To tyrannous hate! Swell, bosom, with thy fraught,
For 'tis of aspics' tongues!

I am getting rid of all of my love for Desdemona.
It's gone.
Come to me, vengeance!
My Love, give up your spot in my life
To Hate instead! O, my chest, fill with pain
As if you are full of snakes' tongues!

IAGO
Yet be content.

Please, be calm.

OTHELLO
O, blood, blood, blood!

O, blood!

IAGO
Patience, I say; your mind perhaps may change.

Be patient. Your mind might change.

OTHELLO
Never, Iago: Like to the Pontic sea,
Whose icy current and compulsive course
Ne'er feels retiring ebb, but keeps due on
To the Propontic and the Hellespont,
Even so my bloody thoughts, with violent pace,
Shall ne'er look back, ne'er ebb to humble love,
Till that a capable and wide revenge
Swallow them up. Now, by yond marble heaven,
Kneels
In the due reverence of a sacred vow
I here engage my words.

No, Iago, never. Like a river to the sea
Whose cold stream and steady course
Never fades away but continues on
To the seas in front of it,
So too my revengeful thoughts violently
never look back or calm to love
Until a they are able to have their full revenge
And let that swallow them up. Now, I swear by the sky

In a sacred, holy vow,
To make my words lead to action.

IAGO
Do not rise yet.
Kneels
Witness, you ever-burning lights above,
You elements that clip us round about,
Witness that here Iago doth give up
The execution of his wit, hands, heart,
To wrong'd Othello's service! Let him command,

And to obey shall be in me remorse,
What bloody business ever.
They rise

Do not get up yet.

Heaven, be my witness,
Everything that surrounds us daily,
Witness that I, Iago, give up
The power of my mind, my hands, and my heart
To Othello who has been wronged! Let him
command,
And I will obey him,
No matter what happens.

OTHELLO
I greet thy love,
Not with vain thanks, but with acceptance
bounteous,
And will upon the instant put thee to't:
Within these three days let me hear thee say
That Cassio's not alive.

- thank you for your love,
Not vainly, but with devoted acceptance.

This instant I will task you:
Within the next three days, I must hear you say
That Cassio is no longer alive.

IAGO
My friend is dead; 'tis done at your request:

But let her live.

OTHELLO
Damn her, lewd minx! O, damn her!
Come, go with me apart; I will withdraw,
To furnish me with some swift means of death
For the fair devil. Now art thou my lieutenant.

IAGO
I am your own for ever.
Exeunt

*My friend will die. At your request it will be
done,*
But let her live.

Damn her, evil whore! O, damn her!
Go away from me. I will withdraw to my room
To figure out some way to kill
That beautiful demon. You are my lieutenant.

I am yours forever.

Scene IV. Before the castle.

Enter DESDEMONA, EMILIA, and Clown

DESDEMONA
Do you know, sirrah, where Lieutenant Cassio lies?

Do you know, sir, where Cassio lies?

Clown
I dare not say he lies any where.

I would not say he lies anywhere.

DESDEMONA
Why, man?

Why would you say that?

Clown
He's a soldier, and for one to say a soldier lies,
is stabbing.

*Because he is a soldier, and one who says that
soldier lie might be stabbed.*

DESDEMONA
Go to: where lodges he?

Come on now, where does he stay?

Clown
To tell you where he lodges, is to tell you where I lie.

*To tell you where he stays is the same as
telling you where I lie.*

DESDEMONA
Can any thing be made of this?

What does this mean?

Clown
I know not where he lodges, and for me to devise a
lodging and say he lies here or he lies there, were
to lie in mine own throat.

*I do not know where he stays, so to say that he
stays anywhere, here or there, is the same
as lying.*

DESDEMONA
Can you inquire him out, and be edified by report?

*Can you ask about him, and report back to
me?*

Clown
I will catechise the world for him; that is, make
questions, and by them answer.

I will ask the world about him.

DESDEMONA
Seek him, bid him come hither: tell him I have

moved my lord on his behalf, and hope all will be well.

*Find him and ask him to come to me. Tell him
that I have
influenced Othello to take him back and that I
hope all will be well.*

Clown
To do this is within the compass of man's wit: and
therefore I will attempt the doing it.
Exit

*This is within my intelligence, and
therefore I will do it.*

DESDEMONA
Where should I lose that handkerchief, Emilia?

Where did I lose my handkerchief, Emilia?

EMILIA
I know not, madam.

I don't know, madam.

DESDEMONA
Believe me, I had rather have lost my purse
Full of crusadoes: and, but my noble Moor

*Believe me, I would have rather lost my purse
Full of money. It's a good thing that the noble Moor*

Is true of mind and made of no such baseness
As jealous creatures are, it were enough

*Is so honest and not made of such evilness
As jealous men are – or else that would be enough*

To put him to ill thinking.

To make him think awful things.

EMILIA
Is he not jealous?

He does not get jealous?

DESDEMONA
Who, he? I think the sun where he was born

Who, Othello? I think the sun where he was born was so hot

Drew all such humours from him.

That it sapped him from those feelings.

EMILIA
Look, where he comes.

Look, here he comes.

DESDEMONA
I will not leave him now till Cassio
Be call'd to him.
Enter OTHELLO
How is't with you, my lord?

*I will not leave him until he calls Cassio
To him.*

How are you, my lord?

OTHELLO
Well, my good lady.

I am well, good lady.

Aside
O, hardness to dissemble!--
How do you, Desdemona?

*It is so hard to pretend! –
How are you, Desdemona?*

DESDEMONA
Well, my good lord.

I am well, my lord.

OTHELLO
Give me your hand: this hand is moist, my lady.

Give me your hand – it is moist with love, my lady.

DESDEMONA
It yet hath felt no age nor known no sorrow.

It has gotten old and has not been sad at all.

OTHELLO
This argues fruitfulness and liberal heart:

This hand says that you have a giving heart and are fertile.

Hot, hot, and moist: this hand of yours requires
A sequester from liberty, fasting and prayer,
Much castigation, exercise devout;
For here's a young and sweating devil here,
That commonly rebels. 'Tis a good hand,

A frank one.

DESDEMONA
You may, indeed, say so;
For 'twas that hand that gave away my heart.

OTHELLO
A liberal hand: the hearts of old gave hands;
But our new heraldry is hands, not hearts.

DESDEMONA
I cannot speak of this. Come now, your promise.

OTHELLO
What promise, chuck?

DESDEMONA
I have sent to bid Cassio come speak with you.

OTHELLO
I have a salt and sorry rheum offends me;
Lend me thy handkerchief.

DESDEMONA
Here, my lord.

OTHELLO
That which I gave you.

DESDEMONA
I have it not about me.

OTHELLO
Not?

DESDEMONA
No, indeed, my lord.

OTHELLO
That is a fault.
That handkerchief
Did an Egyptian to my mother give;
She was a charmer, and could almost read
The thoughts of people: she told her, while
she kept it,

Hot, hot and moist – with a hand like this you need to
Take a break from freedom. You need to fast and pray
And become devout,
Since a young, horny devil could be near,
One that rebels against their devotion. This is a good
hand,
An honest one.

You are right –
This hand gave you my heart.

A free hand – long ago, hearts gave hands,
But now people give each other their hands, but not
their hearts.

I have nothing to say about that. Now then, you have
a promise for me.

What promise, dear?

I have sent away to ask Cassio to speak with you.

I have a cold and a cough bothers me –
Can you lend me your handkerchief?

Here it is, my lord.

The one I gave you, I mean.

I don't have it with me.

No?

No, I don't, my lord.

This is not good.
That handkerchief
Was given to my mother by an Egyptian –
She was a magician and could almost read
People's thoughts. She told her, while she kept it,

'Twould make her amiable and subdue my father
Entirely to her love, but if she lost it
Or made gift of it, my father's eye
Should hold her loathed and his spirits should hunt
After new fancies: she, dying, gave it me;

And bid me, when my fate would have me wive,
To give it her. I did so: and take heed on't;
Make it a darling like your precious eye;
To lose't or give't away were such perdition
As nothing else could match.

DESDEMONA
Is't possible?

OTHELLO
'Tis true: there's magic in the web of it:
A sibyl, that had number'd in the world
The sun to course two hundred compasses,
In her prophetic fury sew'd the work;
The worms were hallow'd that did breed the silk;
And it was dyed in mummy which the skilful
Conserved of maidens' hearts.

DESDEMONA
Indeed! is't true?

OTHELLO
Most veritable; therefore look to't well.

DESDEMONA
Then would to God that I had never seen't!

OTHELLO
Ha! wherefore?

DESDEMONA
Why do you speak so startingly and rash?

OTHELLO
Is't lost? is't gone? speak, is it out
o' the way?

DESDEMONA
Heaven bless us!

OTHELLO
Say you?

DESDEMONA
It is not lost; but what an if it were?

---

*That it would make her obedient to my father
Entirely, but that if she ever lost it
Or gave it away, my father
Would hate her and his desires would hunt
After other women. When she was dying, she gave it to me
And told me that when I found a wife,
To give it to her. I did, so look:
Treat it like your own child to your eye;
To lose it or give it away is a sin
That nothing could match.*

Is that true?

*Yes, there is magic in its threads.
A witch, who had lived in the world
For two hundred years
Sewed it in a prophetic fury.
She used holy worms for the silk
And it was dyed in the mummified
preserves of virgins' hearts.*

Really! It's true?

Yes, very true. So keep an eye on it.

Then I wish I had never seen it!

Ha! Why do you say that?

Why do you speak so aggressively?

*Is it lost? Gone? Tell me, is it
no longer here?*

Heaven help me!

What are you saying?

It is not lost, but what if it was?

OTHELLO
How!

How!

DESDEMONA
I say, it is not lost.

I will say it again, it's not lost.

OTHELLO
Fetch't, let me see't.

Then get it and let me see it.

DESDEMONA
Why, so I can, sir, but I will not now.
This is a trick to put me from my suit:
Pray you, let Cassio be received again.

Well I could, but I will not now.
This is a trick to keep me from my request.
Please, let Cassio be reinstated.

OTHELLO
Fetch me the handkerchief: my mind misgives.

Please get the handkerchief, my mind doubts.

DESDEMONA
Come, come;
You'll never meet a more sufficient man.

Come, now.
You will never meet a more able soldier.

OTHELLO
The handkerchief!

The handkerchief!

DESDEMONA
I pray, talk me of Cassio.

Please, talk to me about Cassio.

OTHELLO
The handkerchief!

The handkerchief!

DESDEMONA
A man that all his time
Hath founded his good fortunes on your love,
Shared dangers with you,--

He has spent all his time
Centering himself on his love for you,
And even went through dangerous situations with
you–

OTHELLO
The handkerchief!

The handkerchief!

DESDEMONA
In sooth, you are to blame.

Truly, you are to blame for acting poorly.

OTHELLO
Away!
Exit

Go away!

EMILIA
Is not this man jealous?

And you said this man is not jealous?

DESDEMONA
I ne'er saw this before.

I never saw him act like this before.

Sure, there's some wonder in this handkerchief:

I am most unhappy in the loss of it.

EMILIA
'Tis not a year or two shows us a man:

They are all but stomachs, and we all but food;
To eat us hungerly, and when they are full,

They belch us. Look you, Cassio and my husband!
Enter CASSIO and IAGO

IAGO
There is no other way; 'tis she must do't:
And, lo, the happiness! go, and importune her.

DESDEMONA
How now, good Cassio! what's the news with you?

CASSIO
Madam, my former suit: I do beseech you
That by your virtuous means I may again
Exist, and be a member of his love
Whom I with all the office of my heart
Entirely honour: I would not be delay'd.
If my offence be of such mortal kind
That nor my service past, nor present sorrows,

Nor purposed merit in futurity,
Can ransom me into his love again,
But to know so must be my benefit;
So shall I clothe me in a forced content,
And shut myself up in some other course,

To fortune's alms.

DESDEMONA
Alas, thrice-gentle Cassio!
My advocation is not now in tune;
My lord is not my lord; nor should I know him,
Were he in favour as in humour alter'd.
So help me every spirit sanctified,
As I have spoken for you all my best
And stood within the blank of his displeasure

For my free speech! you must awhile be patient:
What I can do I will; and more I will
Than for myself I dare: let that suffice you.

But yes, there is something special about the handkerchief.
I am very upset that I lost it.

Only a year or two will truly teach you about a man.
They are all desire, and we are all they desire-
They want to take us, and then when they are satisfied,
They treat us poorly. Here is Cassio and Iago!

There is no other way – she must help you.
And here she is, what luck! Go and beg her.

How are you, good Cassio! What is the news?

Madam, only my previous case. I beg you
That from your friendship that I may again
Return and enter into Othello's love,
Who I with all of my heart
Honor – I do not want to wait longer.
If what I have done is so horrible
That neither my past service nor present sorrows
Nor my future potential merit
Can win me back to him,
Then it would be best that I know.
I will force myself to accept it,
And will stop myself from looking for another way
To regain this fortune.

Oh, gentle Cassio!
My pleading is not working.
Othello is not acting like himself,
But as if he has been changed.
So God must help me,
For I have spoken to you as best I cant
And have stood in front of him as he showed how displeased he was
At my words! You must be patient:
Whatever I can do I will do, more than
I should dare. Let that be enough for you now.

IAGO
Is my lord angry?

Is Othello angry?

EMILIA
He went hence but now,
And certainly in strange unquietness.

He just left,
And certainly seemed like he was in an unsettled
mood.

IAGO
Can he be angry? I have seen the cannon,
When it hath blown his ranks into the air,
And, like the devil, from his very arm
Puff'd his own brother:--and can he be angry?
Something of moment then: I will go meet him:

There's matter in't indeed, if he be angry.

Can he really be angry? I have seen the cannon
Blow his men into the air
And, like the devil, even
Kill his own brother – and he is angry now?
It must be from something important. I will go see
him.
There must be something serious if he is indeed
angry.

DESDEMONA
I prithee, do so.
Exit IAGO
Something, sure, of state,
Either from Venice, or some unhatch'd practice
Made demonstrable here in Cyprus to him,
Hath puddled his clear spirit: and in such cases
Men's natures wrangle with inferior things,
Though great ones are their object. 'Tis even so;

For let our finger ache, and it indues
Our other healthful members even to that sense
Of pain: nay, we must think men are not gods,
Nor of them look for such observances
As fit the bridal. Beshrew me much, Emilia,
I was, unhandsome warrior as I am,
Arraigning his unkindness with my soul;
But now I find I had suborn'd the witness,
And he's indicted falsely.

Please, do so.

It must be a national item,
Something from Venice, or else some plot
That here in Cyprus he discovered,
And this must have clouded his mind. In such cases,
Men fight with the small, trivial things,
When the more important ones are their true object.
It's true for us too,
When our finger hurts, it makes
The rest of our body align with that pain
And hurt as well. No, we must not think men are gods,
Nor think that they will always act as if
It is their wedding day. O curse me, Emilia,
I am such a poor soldier, and I
Blamed him for his unkindness,
When really I was judging him
And thinking of him wrongly.

EMILIA
Pray heaven it be state-matters, as you think,
And no conception nor no jealous toy
Concerning you.

I pray that it is state matters, like you think,
And no imagination or jealousy
That is about you.

DESDEMONA
Alas the day! I never gave him cause.

I would rue that day! I never gave him a reason for
such thoughts.

EMILIA
But jealous souls will not be answer'd so;
They are not ever jealous for the cause,
But jealous for they are jealous: 'tis a monster
Begot upon itself, born on itself.

But jealous men do not need reason.
They are not jealous for a cause,
But simply because they are jealous. It's a monster
That creates itself.

DESDEMONA
Heaven keep that monster from Othello's mind!

God, keep that monster away from Othello!

EMILIA
Lady, amen.

Amen to that.

DESDEMONA
I will go seek him. Cassio, walk hereabout:
If I do find him fit, I'll move your suit

And seek to effect it to my uttermost.

I will go to him. Cassio, stay here –
If I find him able to talk to, I will plead your case
With all my strength.

CASSIO
I humbly thank your ladyship.
Exeunt DESDEMONA and EMILIA
Enter BIANCA

I humbly thank you.

BIANCA
Save you, friend Cassio!

Hello, Cassio!

CASSIO
What make you from home?
How is it with you, my most fair Bianca?
I' faith, sweet love, I was coming to your house.

How are you so far from home?
How are you, my beautiful Bianca?
Truly, sweet love, I was on my way to you.

BIANCA
And I was going to your lodging, Cassio.
What, keep a week away? seven days and nights?

Eight score eight hours? and lovers' absent hours,

More tedious than the dial eight score times?
O weary reckoning!

And I was on my way to your house, Cassio.
What, should I stay away from you for a full week? Seven days and nights?
One hundred and sixty eight hours? And these are the hours of lovers apart,
Which are much longer than regular ones.
O what a tedious waiting!

CASSIO
Pardon me, Bianca:
I have this while with leaden thoughts been press'd:
But I shall, in a more continuate time,
Strike off this score of absence. Sweet Bianca,
Giving her DESDEMONA's handkerchief
Take me this work out.

Forgive me, Bianca –
I have been depressed with heavy thoughts,
But hopefully I will soon
Make up this absent time. Sweet Bianca,

Could you copy this pattern for me?

BIANCA
O Cassio, whence came this?
This is some token from a newer friend:
To the felt absence now I feel a cause:
Is't come to this? Well, well.

Cassio, where did this come from?
This must be a gift from a newer girl.
Now I know why you were absent.
Has it come to this?

CASSIO
Go to, woman!

Go do it, woman!

Throw your vile guesses in the devil's teeth,

From whence you have them. You are jealous now
That this is from some mistress, some remembrance:
No, in good troth, Bianca.

BIANCA
Why, whose is it?

CASSIO
I know not, sweet: I found it in my chamber.
I like the work well: ere it be demanded--

As like enough it will--I'ld have it copied:

Take it, and do't; and leave me for this time.

BIANCA
Leave you! wherefore?

CASSIO
I do attend here on the general;
And think it no addition, nor my wish,
To have him see me woman'd.

BIANCA
Why, I pray you?

CASSIO
Not that I love you not.

BIANCA
But that you do not love me.
I pray you, bring me on the way a little,
And say if I shall see you soon at night.

CASSIO
'Tis but a little way that I can bring you;
For I attend here: but I'll see you soon.

BIANCA
'Tis very good; I must be circumstanced.
Exeunt

Get rid of your evil guesses and send them back
To where you got them. You are jealous
That this is from some new mistress of mine:
It's not, truly, Bianca.

Then whose is it?

I don't know, my sweet. I found it in my room.
I like the stitching, and before I have to give it back –
Which I certainly will – I would like to have it copied for me.
Take it and stitch it for me, and leave me for now.

Leave you! Why?

I am waiting here for Othello,
And I do not think it will help me
If he sees me with a woman.

Why?

Though I do love you.

But you don't love me.
Please, bring me along with you
And tell me if I will see you later.

I can only bring you a little ways
Since I must wait here. I will see you soon.

Alright, fine. I will obey the circumstance.

Act IV

Scene I. Cyprus. Before the castle.

Enter OTHELLO and IAGO

IAGO
Will you think so?

Do you think so?

OTHELLO
Think so, Iago!

Think so! Iago!

IAGO
What,
To kiss in private?

What,
Did they kiss in private?

OTHELLO
An unauthorized kiss.

A wrong, secret kiss.

IAGO
Or to be naked with her friend in bed
An hour or more, not meaning any harm?

Or perhaps they were naked together in bed
For an hour or so, but didn't do anything?

OTHELLO
Naked in bed, Iago, and not mean harm!
It is hypocrisy against the devil:

They that mean virtuously, and yet do so,

The devil their virtue tempts, and they tempt heaven.

Naked in bed, and not do anything! Absurd!
That would be like the devil being a hypocrite
and not really doing evil.
If they meant to not have sex, and yet laid
together like that,
Then they are asking to be tempted, and
condemned.

IAGO
So they do nothing, 'tis a venial slip:

But if I give my wife a handkerchief, --

Then if they do not do anything, it is only a
minor slip-up.
But, if I give my wife a handkerchief—

OTHELLO
What then?

Then what?

IAGO
Why, then, 'tis hers, my lord; and, being hers,

She may, I think, bestow't on any man.

Well, then it is hers, my lord. And since it is
hers,
She can give it to anyone.

OTHELLO
She is protectress of her honour too:
May she give that?

She is also the owner of her honor, though –
Can she give that to anyone?

IAGO
Her honour is an essence that's not seen;
They have it very oft that have it not:

But, for the handkerchief,--

Her honor is a quality, not a tangible object.
Many times people do not even have the honor
they think they do.
But a handkerchief—

OTHELLO
By heaven, I would most gladly have forgot it.
Thou said'st, it comes o'er my memory,
As doth the raven o'er the infected house,

Boding to all--he had my handkerchief.

IAGO
Ay, what of that?

OTHELLO
That's not so good now.

IAGO
What,
If I had said I had seen him do you wrong?

Or heard him say,--as knaves be such abroad,
Who having, by their own importunate suit,

Or voluntary dotage of some mistress,
Convinced or supplied them, cannot choose

But they must blab--

OTHELLO
Hath he said any thing?

IAGO
He hath, my lord; but be you well assured,
No more than he'll unswear.

OTHELLO
What hath he said?

IAGO
'Faith, that he did--I know not what he did.

OTHELLO
What? what?

IAGO
Lie--

OTHELLO
With her?

IAGO
With her, on her; what you will.

By God, I wish I could forget about it
What you said clouds my thinking
And, like a raven flying over a cursed house,
Foreshadows evil. He has my handkerchief!

So, what of it?

That is no good.

Well
What if I said that I had seen him do something wrong?
Or if I heard him say – like evil men,
Who of their own forceful manipulation
Or the love of some woman
Get what they are after, cannot help themselves
But talk about it–

Did he say something?

He did, my lord, but you should know
That he will only deny it.

What did he say?

Well, that he did– I don't know what he did.

What? Tell me.

That he laid

With her?

With her, on her, whatever you think.

OTHELLO
Lie with her! lie on her! We say lie on her, when

they belie her. Lie with her! that's fulsome.

--Handkerchief--confessions--handkerchief!—To

confess, and be hanged for his labour;--first, to be

hanged, and then to confess.--I tremble at it.

Nature would not invest herself in such shadowing
passion without some instruction. It is not words

that shake me thus. Pish! Noses, ears, and lips.

--Is't possible?--Confess--handkerchief!--O devil!--

Falls in a trance

IAGO
Work on,
My medicine, work! Thus credulous fools are caught;

And many worthy and chaste dames even thus,
All guiltless, meet reproach. What, ho! my lord!

My lord, I say! Othello!
Enter CASSIO
How now, Cassio!

CASSIO
What's the matter?

IAGO
My lord is fall'n into an epilepsy:
This is his second fit; he had one yesterday.

CASSIO
Rub him about the temples.

IAGO
No, forbear;
The lethargy must have his quiet course:
If not, he foams at mouth and by and by
Breaks out to savage madness. Look he stirs:
Do you withdraw yourself a little while,
He will recover straight: when he is gone,
I would on great occasion speak with you.
Exit CASSIO

*Lay with her! On her! I would rather hear,
instead of "lie on her"
that people were lying about her. Lay with
her! That's disgusting.
–Handkerchief–confessions–handkerchief! He
must
confess and then be hung for his confession. –
No, first
hung, and then he can confess. – I am shaking
with anger.
Nature would not let me feel like this, in such
passion, if there was no truth to the matter.
Simple words
can't shake me like this. Bah! Noses, ears,
lips.
Is it possible? – Confess – handkerchief! – O
devil!*

*Keep going,
My poisonous imaginations that I gave him!
Naively trusting fools are easily caught
And many worthy, pure women are,
Even though they are blameless, punished.
What, Othello!
Othello!*

Hello, Cassio!

What is going on?

*Othello has fallen into an epileptic fit.
This is his second one – the first one was
yesterday.*

Rub his temples.

*No, just wait –
The fit should run its course.
If it doesn't, he begins to foam at the mouth
And become mad. Look, he wakes.
Go away for a little while,
He will recover quickly. When he is gone,
I greatly need to talk to you.*

How is it, general? have you not hurt your head?

General, how are you? Did you hurt your head?

OTHELLO
Dost thou mock me?

Are you mocking me?

IAGO
I mock you! no, by heaven.
Would you would bear your fortune like a man!

Mocking you! Of course not.
But I wish you could bear your misfortune like a man!

OTHELLO
A horned man's a monster and a beast.

A man who has been cheated on is more of a monster and an animal.

IAGO
There's many a beast then in a populous city,

And many a civil monster.

Well there are many animals, then, in a crowded city,
And many monsters are still polite.

OTHELLO
Did he confess it?

Did he confess to it?

IAGO
Good sir, be a man;
Think every bearded fellow that's but yoked
May draw with you: there's millions now alive

That nightly lie in those unproper beds

Which they dare swear peculiar: your case is better.

O, 'tis the spite of hell, the fiend's arch-mock,

To lip a wanton in a secure couch,
And to suppose her chaste! No, let me know;

And knowing what I am, I know what she shall be.

Good sir, act like a man.
Every married fellow
Has the same situation you do. There are millions
Who go to bed each night with their cheating wives
Whom they think are loyal to them. Your situation is better.
O, it is indeed a curse, the worst kind of mocking,
To kiss a loose woman
And believe she is pure! No, I would rather know,
And then I will know what I really am and what she really is.

OTHELLO
O, thou art wise; 'tis certain.

You are certainly wise.

IAGO
Stand you awhile apart;
Confine yourself but in a patient list.
Whilst you were here o'erwhelmed with your grief--

A passion most unsuiting such a man--
Cassio came hither: I shifted him away,
And laid good 'scuse upon your ecstasy,
Bade him anon return and here speak with me;
The which he promised. Do but encave yourself,
And mark the fleers, the gibes, and notable scorns,

Go away from the situation for a little
And calm down in patience.
While you were overwhelmed here in a fit of sadness –
Which is not the proper response for a man –
Cassio came here. I ushered him away
And made up an excuse for your fit,
But asked him to come back and talk with me,
Which he agreed to do. So hide yourself
And make a note of all of the sneers and scorns

That dwell in every region of his face;
For I will make him tell the tale anew,
Where, how, how oft, how long ago, and when
He hath, and is again to cope your wife:
I say, but mark his gesture. Marry, patience;
Or I shall say you are all in all in spleen,
And nothing of a man.

OTHELLO
Dost thou hear, Iago?
I will be found most cunning in my patience;
But--dost thou hear?--most bloody.

IAGO
That's not amiss;
But yet keep time in all. Will you withdraw?
OTHELLO retires
Now will I question Cassio of Bianca,
A housewife that by selling her desires
Buys herself bread and clothes: it is a creature
That dotes on Cassio; as 'tis the strumpet's plague
To beguile many and be beguiled by one:

He, when he hears of her, cannot refrain

From the excess of laughter. Here he comes:
Re-enter CASSIO
As he shall smile, Othello shall go mad;
And his unbookish jealousy must construe
Poor Cassio's smiles, gestures and light behavior,
Quite in the wrong. How do you now, lieutenant?

CASSIO
The worser that you give me the addition
Whose want even kills me.

IAGO
Ply Desdemona well, and you are sure on't.
Speaking lower
Now, if this suit lay in Bianca's power,
How quickly should you speed!

CASSIO
Alas, poor caitiff!

OTHELLO
Look, how he laughs already!

IAGO
I never knew woman love man so.

That will show up on his face.
I will make him tell the story again –
Where, how, how often, when it started, and when
He plans again to go to your wife.
Again, make a note of his actions. Be patient,
Or I will think that you are taken up by your rage
And not really a man.

Do you hear me, Iago?
I will be quiet and cunning in my patience,
But – and hear this – still very violent when the time comes.

That's not a wrong thing,
But it must be in the right time. Now go away.

I will ask Cassio about Bianca,
A prostitute that sells sex
So that she can buy food and clothes. She
Loves Cassio – it is the loose woman's curse
To convince many to love her, but to be in love with one.
When he hears talk about her, he won't be able to stop
Laughing. Here he comes.

He will smile, and Othello will go crazy.
His unhinged jealousy will interpret
Cassio's smiles, actions, and happy behavior
Wrongly. How are you, lieutenant?

I am worse when you call me by that rank
Since I want it back so badly.

Beg Desdemona well, and you will get it.

Now if it were up to Bianca,
You would have it back so quickly!

Ah, poor awful woman.

Look how he laughs!

I never knew a woman who was so in love with a man.

CASSIO
Alas, poor rogue! I think, i' faith, she loves me.

That poor rogue! I think that she really does love me.

OTHELLO
Now he denies it faintly, and laughs it out.

Now he denies it quietly and tries to laugh it away.

IAGO
Do you hear, Cassio?

Have you heard this, Cassio?

OTHELLO
Now he importunes him
To tell it o'er: go to; well said, well said.

*Now Iago is asking him
To tell the story again. Well played.*

IAGO
She gives it out that you shall marry hey:
Do you intend it?

*She says that you are to marry –
Do you intend to do this?*

CASSIO
Ha, ha, ha!

Ha ha ha!

OTHELLO
Do you triumph, Roman? do you triumph?

Do you think you have won, really?

CASSIO
I marry her! what? a customer! Prithee, bear some

charity to my wit: do not think it so unwholesome.

Ha, ha, ha!

*I marry her! What? I am only a customer! Please, give
my intelligence some credit – I am not that dumb.
Ha ha ha!*

OTHELLO
So, so, so, so: they laugh that win.

Well, well, well – the true winner has the last laugh.

IAGO
'Faith, the cry goes that you shall marry her.

Really! The word is that you are going to marry her.

CASSIO
Prithee, say true.

Please, speak honestly.

IAGO
I am a very villain else.

I am, and would be a villain to say otherwise.

OTHELLO
Have you scored me? Well.

Have you made her pregnant as well? Fine.

CASSIO
This is the monkey's own giving out: she is
persuaded I will marry her, out of her own love and

flattery, not out of my promise.

*Then this is made up by her, that monkey. She
thinks I will marry her because she loves me and
flatters herself, but it is not backed up by me.*

OTHELLO
Iago beckons me; now he begins the story.

Iago is motioning that Cassio is beginning the story.

CASSIO
She was here even now; she haunts me in
every place.
I was the other day talking on the sea-bank with
certain Venetians; and thither comes the bauble,
and, by this hand, she falls me thus about my
neck--

She was just here – she follows me everywhere.

*The other day I was talking on the shore with
a few Venetians and here comes that fool,
takes me by the hand, and puts her arms around me
like this–*

OTHELLO
Crying 'O dear Cassio!' as it were: his gesture
imports it.

*It looks like he is motioning how she cried out his
name.*

CASSIO
So hangs, and lolls, and weeps upon me; so hales,

and pulls me: ha, ha, ha!

*She hangs on me, and cries over me, and shakes me
like this,
and pulls on me like this. Ha ha ha!*

OTHELLO
Now he tells how she plucked him to my
chamber. O,
I see that nose of yours, but not that dog I shall
throw it to.

Now he is telling how she took him to my room. O,

*I see your nose, but I cannot yet see the dog that I will
throw it to.*

CASSIO
Well, I must leave her company.

Well, I must stay away from her.

IAGO
Before me! look, where she comes.

Then look out, for here she comes.

CASSIO
'Tis such another fitchew! marry a perfumed one.
Enter BIANCA
What do you mean by this haunting of me?

It's a whore like all of the others, wearing perfume.

Why do you keep following me?

BIANCA
Let the devil and his dam haunt you!
What did you
mean by that same handkerchief you gave me
even now?
I was a fine fool to take it. I must take out the
work?--A likely piece of work, that you should
find
it in your chamber, and not know who left it
there!
This is some minx's token, and I must take
out the work?
There; give it your hobby-horse: wheresoever
you had it, I'll take out no work on't.

I hope the devil and his wife haunt you! Why did

you give me that handkerchief earlier?

*I was a fool to take it. And I must copy it for you?
A likely story, that you would find it*

in your room and not know who put it there!

*This is some token from another woman, and you
want me to copy it?
There, take it, give it back to the other woman
For I will not copy it for you.*

CASSIO
How now, my sweet Bianca! how now! how now!

Oh don't be like that, sweet Bianca!

OTHELLO
By heaven, that should be my handkerchief!

By God, that is my handkerchief!

BIANCA
An you'll come to supper to-night, you may; an you

If you want to have dinner with me tonight, you may.

will not, come when you are next prepared for.

If you do not want to, then come some other time.

Exit

IAGO
After her, after her.

Go after her.

CASSIO
'Faith, I must; she'll rail in the street else.

Truly, I must or else she will scream in the streets.

IAGO
Will you sup there?

Will you eat there tonight?

CASSIO
'Faith, I intend so.

Yes, I think so.

IAGO
Well, I may chance to see you; for I would very fain
speak with you.

Well I might see you then. I would very much like to speak with you.

CASSIO
Prithee, come; will you?

Please do come.

IAGO
Go to; say no more.
Exit CASSIO

Go after her and say no more now.

OTHELLO
[Advancing] How shall I murder him, Iago?

How should I kill him, Iago?

IAGO
Did you perceive how he laughed at his vice?

So you saw how he laughed at his sins?

OTHELLO
O Iago!

O Iago!

IAGO
And did you see the handkerchief?

Did you see the handkerchief?

OTHELLO
Was that mine?

Was that mine?

IAGO
Yours by this hand: and to see how he prizes the
foolish woman your wife! she gave it him, and he
hath given it his whore.

*Yes, yours. And you can see how highly he prizes
your foolish wife, for she gave it to him and he
gave it to his whore.*

OTHELLO
I would have him nine years a-killing.
A fine woman! a fair woman! a sweet woman!

*I would like to kill him for nine years straight.
She is such a fine, sweet woman!*

IAGO
Nay, you must forget that.

No, forget about that.

OTHELLO
Ay, let her rot, and perish, and be damned
to-night;
for she shall not live: no, my heart is turned to

stone; I strike it, and it hurts my hand. O, the
world hath not a sweeter creature: she might
lie by
an emperor's side and command him tasks.

Yes, she can rot and die and be damned,

*because she will no longer live. No, my heart has
turned
to stone and it hurts my hand when I hit it. The
world has not seen a sweeter woman – she could
sleep
with the emperor himself and still tell him what to do.*

IAGO
Nay, that's not your way.

No, that is not who you are.

OTHELLO
Hang her! I do but say what she is: so delicate

with her needle: an admirable musician: O! she
will sing the savageness out of a bear: of so high
and plenteous wit and invention:--

*Damn her! I am only saying what she is in reality.
She
is a good seamstress and a wonderful musician – she
could calm a bear with her voice – and she has such
a clever mind –*

IAGO
She's the worse for all this.

All the worse that she ended up like this.

OTHELLO
O, a thousand thousand times: and then, of so
gentle a condition!

*A thousand times worse – O and she has
such a sweet personality.*

IAGO
Ay, too gentle.

Too sweet, perhaps.

OTHELLO
Nay, that's certain: but yet the pity of it, Iago!
O Iago, the pity of it, Iago!

*True, but that's the sadness of it, Iago!
Iago, how sad, Iago!*

IAGO
If you are so fond over her iniquity, give her

patent to offend; for, if it touch not you, it comes

*If you love her so much even when she cheats on you,
then give her
permission to keep doing it. If it does not bother you,
it won't be an issue*

near nobody.

OTHELLO
I will chop her into messes: cuckold me!

I will chop her into bits! How dare she cheat on me!

IAGO
O, 'tis foul in her.

It's very evil.

OTHELLO
With mine officer!

With my own officer!

IAGO
That's fouler.

Even worse.

OTHELLO
Get me some poison, Iago; this night: I'll not
expostulate with her, lest her body and beauty
unprovide my mind again: this night, Iago.

*Iago, get me some poison tonight. I will not
argue at all with her so that her beauty
cannot tempt me to change my mind Tonight,
Iago.*

IAGO
Do it not with poison, strangle her in her bed, even

the bed she hath contaminated.

*Don't do it with poison, but strangle her in
her bed, the same
one that she ruined.*

OTHELLO
Good, good: the justice of it pleases: very good.

Yes, I appreciate the fitting justice of it.

IAGO
And for Cassio, let me be his undertaker: you
shall hear more by midnight.

*As for Cassio, leave him to me. You
Will hear from me by midnight.*

OTHELLO
Excellent good.
A trumpet within
What trumpet is that same?

Excellent.

What trumpet is that?

IAGO
Something from Venice, sure. 'Tis Lodovico

Come from the duke: and, see, your wife is with him.

*It sounds like someone from Venice. It is
Lodovico
Sent from the duke – and look, your wife is
with him.*

Enter LODOVICO, DESDEMONA, and Attendants

LODOVICO
Save you, worthy general!

God bless you, worthy General!

OTHELLO
With all my heart, sir.

And all of us, sir.

LODOVICO
The duke and senators of Venice greet you.

The duke and senators from Venice send their greetings.

Gives him a letter

OTHELLO
I kiss the instrument of their pleasures.
Opens the letter, and reads

I will gladly read and obey their requests.

DESDEMONA
And what's the news, good cousin Lodovico?

What is the news, good cousin Lodovico?

IAGO
I am very glad to see you, signior.
Welcome to Cyprus.

I am glad to see you, sir.
Welcome to Cyprus.

LODOVICO
I thank you. How does Lieutenant Cassio?

Thank you, How is Lieutenant Cassio?

IAGO
Lives, sir.

Alive, sir.

DESDEMONA
Cousin, there's fall'n between him and my lord

Cousin, there has been a falling out between him and my lord.

An unkind breach: but you shall make all well.

It's an awful thing, but you will fix it.

OTHELLO
Are you sure of that?

Are you sure?

DESDEMONA
My lord?

What do you mean, my lord?

OTHELLO
[Reads] 'This fail you not to do, as you will--'

Do not fail to do this, since then you will –

LODOVICO
He did not call; he's busy in the paper.
Is there division 'twixt my lord and Cassio?

He didn't speak, he's reading.
So there has been a fight between Othello and Cassio?

DESDEMONA
A most unhappy one: I would do much
To atone them, for the love I bear to Cassio.

A sad one, yes. I would do whatever I can
To have them forgive each other since I love Cassio.

OTHELLO
Fire and brimstone!

O, damnation!

DESDEMONA
My lord?

Excuse me?

OTHELLO
Are you wise?

Are you sane?

DESDEMONA
What, is he angry?

Wait, is Othello angry?

LODOVICO
May be the letter moved him;
For, as I think, they do command him home,

Deputing Cassio in his government.

Perhaps the letter has upset him.
I think that they are requesting him to come home,
Placing Cassio in charge.

DESDEMONA
Trust me, I am glad on't.

Oh, well that is good news.

OTHELLO
Indeed!

Is it really!

DESDEMONA
My lord?

Othello?

OTHELLO
I am glad to see you mad.

I am glad that you are getting angry.

DESDEMONA
Why, sweet Othello,--

Othello, why?

OTHELLO
[Striking her] Devil!

You devil!

DESDEMONA
I have not deserved this.

I haven't done anything to deserve this.

LODOVICO
My lord, this would not be believed in Venice,
Though I should swear I saw't: 'tis very much:
Make her amends; she weeps.

My lord, no one in Venice would believe this,
Even if I swore that I saw it. This is too much.
Apologize, she is crying.

OTHELLO
O devil, devil!
If that the earth could teem with woman's tears,

Each drop she falls would prove a crocodile.
Out of my sight!

O she is the debil!
The whole earth could be filled with this woman's tears
And I would still believe she is falsely crying.
Get out of my sight!

DESDEMONA
I will not stay to offend you.
Going

I will not stay here to upset you then.

LODOVICO
Truly, an obedient lady:

She is truly an obedient woman.

I do beseech your lordship, call her back.

I beg you, Othello, call her back.

OTHELLO
Mistress!

Madam!

DESDEMONA
My lord?

Yes, my lord?

OTHELLO
What would you with her, sir?

What do you want with her, sir?

LODOVICO
Who, I, my lord?

What do I want?

OTHELLO
Ay; you did wish that I would make her turn:
Sir, she can turn, and turn, and yet go on,
And turn again; and she can weep, sir, weep;
And she's obedient, as you say, obedient,
Very obedient. Proceed you in your tears.
Concerning this, sir,--O well-painted passion!--
I am commanded home. Get you away;
I'll send for you anon. Sir, I obey the mandate,

And will return to Venice. Hence, avaunt!
Exit DESDEMONA
Cassio shall have my place. And, sir, tonight,
I do entreat that we may sup together:
You are welcome, sir, to Cyprus.--Goats and
monkeys!
Exit

Yes, you asked me to have her come back.
She can turn around and around and
Keep turning. She can cry and cry.
And she is so obedient, just as you say,
Very obedient. Go on and cry.
Now about this letter – O what fake crying! –
It commands me to return home. Get away from me,
I will send for you to return soon. Sir, I will obey this order
And return to Venice. Away, go away!

Cassio will take my spot and, sir, tonight,
Please come and eat with me.
You are welcome to Cyprus. –Horny animals everywhere!

LODOVICO
Is this the noble Moor whom our full senate

Call all in all sufficient? Is this the nature

Whom passion could not shake? whose solid virtue
The shot of accident, nor dart of chance,
Could neither graze nor pierce?

Is this the same noble Moor whom everyone in the government
Calls the most able of the soldiers? Is this the same character
That passion could never shake? Whose goodness

No accident or chance misfortune
Could destroy?

IAGO
He is much changed.

He has changed a lot.

LODOVICO
Are his wits safe? is he not light of brain?

Is he still sane? Or has he lost his mind?

IAGO
He's that he is: I may not breathe my censure

He is what he is. I will not voice any criticism

What he might be: if what he might he is not,

I would to heaven he were!

LODOVICO
What, strike his wife!

IAGO
'Faith, that was not so well; yet would I knew
That stroke would prove the worst!

LODOVICO
Is it his use?
Or did the letters work upon his blood,
And new-create this fault?

IAGO
Alas, alas!
It is not honesty in me to speak
What I have seen and known. You shall observe him,

And his own courses will denote him so

That I may save my speech: do but go after,

And mark how he continues.

LODOVICO
I am sorry that I am deceived in him.
Exeunt

About what he might be – if he is not what he should be,
Than I wish he were!

He struck his wife!

Yes, that was not very good. But I wish I knew
That that was the worst thing he could do!

Does he usually do things like that?
Or did the letters make him angry
And lead him to this new sin?

Oh it's so bad!
It is not honest for me to say
What I have seen and known before. You watch him
And his actions will tell you all you need to know so
That I do not have to say anything. But follow him,
And watch his lifestyle.

I am very sad that I was wrong about him.

Scene II. A room in the castle.

Enter OTHELLO and EMILIA

OTHELLO
You have seen nothing then?

So you have not seen anything?

EMILIA
Nor ever heard, nor ever did suspect.

No, and I didn't hear or suspect anything either.

OTHELLO
Yes, you have seen Cassio and she together.

But you did see Cassio with her.

EMILIA
But then I saw no harm, and then I heard

Each syllable that breath made up between them.

But there was nothing wrong there, and I heard
Every word they said between them

OTHELLO
What, did they never whisper?

They never whispered?

EMILIA
Never, my lord.

Never, my lord.

OTHELLO
Nor send you out o' the way?

And never sent you away?

EMILIA
Never.

Never.

OTHELLO
To fetch her fan, her gloves, her mask, nor nothing?

Not to get her fan or gloves or hat or anything?

EMILIA
Never, my lord.

Never, my lord.

OTHELLO
That's strange.

That is very strange.

EMILIA
I durst, my lord, to wager she is honest,
Lay down my soul at stake: if you think other,

Remove your thought; it doth abuse your bosom.
If any wretch have put this in your head,
Let heaven requite it with the serpent's curse!
For, if she be not honest, chaste, and true,
There's no man happy; the purest of their wives

My lord, I think she is very honest
And would bet my soul on it. If you think otherwise,
Please rethink it – it ruins your credibility.
Whoever has put this into your head,
May heaven curse his head!
If Desdemona is not honest, pure, and true,
Than no man may ever be happy. The purest of their wives

Is foul as slander.

Are then evil.

OTHELLO
Bid her come hither: go.
Exit EMILIA
She says enough; yet she's a simple bawd

That cannot say as much. This is a subtle whore,

A closet lock and key of villanous secrets

And yet she'll kneel and pray; I have seen her do't.

Enter DESDEMONA with EMILIA

Please ask her to come to me.

She speaks well for Desdemona – though one would be a stupid prostitute
Who could not lie as well as that. Desdemona is a tricky whore,
She is full of evil secrets that are locked in her,
And all the while she will kneel and pray. I've seen it.

DESDEMONA
My lord, what is your will?

My lord, what do you want?

OTHELLO
Pray, chuck, come hither.

Please, darling, come here.

DESDEMONA
What is your pleasure?

What would you like?

OTHELLO
Let me see your eyes;
Look in my face.

Let me see your eyes,
Look at me.

DESDEMONA
What horrible fancy's this?

What awful game is this.

OTHELLO
[To EMILIA] Some of your function, mistress;
Leave procreants alone and shut the door;
Cough, or cry 'hem,' if any body come:
Your mystery, your mystery: nay, dispatch.
Exit EMILIA

Go to your work, mistress.
Leave us alone to have sex, and shut the door.
Cough or cry out if anyone comes,
Since that is your job. Now, go.

DESDEMONA
Upon my knees, what doth your speech import?
I understand a fury in your words.
But not the words.

I beg you, what do you mean?
There is anger in your words,
But not in the words themselves.

OTHELLO
Why, what art thou?

Who are you?

DESDEMONA
Your wife, my lord; your true
And loyal wife.

Your wife, lord, your honest
And loyal wife.

OTHELLO
Come, swear it, damn thyself
Lest, being like one of heaven, the devils themselves
Should fear to seize thee: therefore be double damn'd:
Swear thou art honest.

Come and swear it to me. Damn yourself by lying
So that the devils will not confuse you for an angel

And thus fail to take you. Be double-damned

And swear your honesty.

DESDEMONA
Heaven doth truly know it.

God knows I am.

OTHELLO
Heaven truly knows that thou art false as hell.

God knows that you have been as evil as hell.

DESDEMONA
To whom, my lord? with whom? how am I false?

To whom, my lord? With whom? How have I been unfaithful?

OTHELLO
O Desdemona! away! away! away!

O Desdemona go away!

DESDEMONA
Alas the heavy day! Why do you weep?
Am I the motive of these tears, my lord?
If haply you my father do suspect
An instrument of this your calling back,
Lay not your blame on me: If you have lost him,
Why, I have lost him too.

This is such a sad day! Why do you weep?
Did I force you to cry, my lord?
If you suspect that my father
Is the reason you have been called back,
Then do not blame me. If he hates you,
Then I hate him too.

OTHELLO
Had it pleased heaven
To try me with affliction; had they rain'd
All kinds of sores and shames on my bare head,
Steep'd me in poverty to the very lips,
Given to captivity me and my utmost hopes,

I should have found in some place of my soul
A drop of patience: but, alas, to make me
A fixed figure for the time of scorn
To point his slow unmoving finger at!
Yet could I bear that too; well, very well:
But there, where I have garner'd up my heart,

Where either I must live, or bear no life;
The fountain from the which my current runs,
Or else dries up; to be discarded thence!
Or keep it as a cistern for foul toads
To knot and gender in! Turn thy complexion there,
Patience, thou young and rose-lipp'd cherubin,--
Ay, there, look grim as hell!

If heaven wanted
To test me through pain, if they had placed
All kinds of sores and illnesses on my body,
Or had made me incredibly poor,
Or had given me to slavery so that I could not even hope for freedom,
I would have found in my soul
An ability to be patient. But instead, He has made me
Into a man built for being mocked
And for others to point their fingers at!
I could even handle that, though,
If it did not have to do with my heart's foundations, my wife,
The person whom I depend on,
And the fountain my lineage must come from,
Or it dries up and is ruined!
Now this fountain is a container for ugly toads
To copulate in! Turn your gaze to this,
O Patience, you young and rose-lipped angel,
Look how awful it is!

DESDEMONA

I hope my noble lord esteems me honest.

I wish my noble lord would know that I am honest.

OTHELLO
O, ay; as summer flies are in the shambles,

That quicken even with blowing. O thou weed,

Who art so lovely fair and smell'st so sweet
That the sense aches at thee, would thou hadst

ne'er been born!

O yes, you are as honest as the summer flies in the woods
That leave each time the wind blows. O you weed,
Who is so beautiful and smell so good,
That one aches to see and smell you – it would be better if
you were never born!

DESDEMONA
Alas, what ignorant sin have I committed?

Please, what sin that I do not know about have I committed?

OTHELLO
Was this fair paper, this most goodly book,

Made to write 'whore' upon? What committed!

Committed! O thou public commoner!
I should make very forges of my cheeks,
That would to cinders burn up modesty,
Did I but speak thy deeds. What committed!
Heaven stops the nose at it and the moon winks,

The bawdy wind that kisses all it meets
Is hush'd within the hollow mine of earth,
And will not hear it. What committed!
Impudent strumpet!

Was this beautiful woman, like a good and holy book,
Created in order for someone to write "whore" on it? What you committed!
Committed! O you public prostitute!
My cheeks would burn like ovens
And devour all modesty in their flames
If I spoke aloud what you did. What you did!
Heaven holds its nose at you, and the moon closes its eyes,
And the playful wind that kisses everything
Has been calmed and quieted into the earth,
And refuses to hear it. What you did!
Bold whore!

DESDEMONA
By heaven, you do me wrong.

By God, you are treating me wrongly.

OTHELLO
Are you not a strumpet?

Aren't you a whore?

DESDEMONA
No, as I am a Christian:
If to preserve this vessel for my lord
From any other foul unlawful touch
Be not to be a strumpet, I am none.

No, I am a Christian,
If I keep my body only for you
And do not allow any evil touch,
If that is the definition of someone who is not a whore, then I am not one.

OTHELLO
What, not a whore?

You aren't a whore?

DESDEMONA
No, as I shall be saved.

No, by my own salvation I swear.

OTHELLO
Is't possible?

Is it possible?

DESDEMONA
O, heaven forgive us!

God forgive us!

OTHELLO
I cry you mercy, then:
I took you for that cunning whore of Venice
That married with Othello.
Raising his voice
You, mistress,
That have the office opposite to Saint Peter,

And keep the gate of hell!
Re-enter EMILIA
You, you, ay, you!
We have done our course; there's money for
your pains:
I pray you, turn the key and keep our counsel.

Exit

I ask for your forgiveness then:
I mistook you for the tricky whore from Venice
Who married Othello.

You, mistress,
That have watched the gates of this room like Saint
Peter's opposite,
Watching the gates of hell!

You, yes, you!
We have finished. Here is money for your work.

Please, lock the door and keep silent about our
conversation.

EMILIA
Alas, what does this gentleman conceive?
How do you, madam? how do you, my good lady?

What is Othello thinking?
Madam, how are you, my lady?

DESDEMONA
'Faith, half asleep.

I am dazed.

EMILIA
Good madam, what's the matter with my lord?

O madam, what is the matter with Othello?

DESDEMONA
With who?

With who?

EMILIA
Why, with my lord, madam.

With your lord, madam.

DESDEMONA
Who is thy lord?

Who is my lord?

EMILIA
He that is yours, sweet lady.

He that belongs to you, sweet lady.

DESDEMONA
I have none: do not talk to me, Emilia;
I cannot weep; nor answer have I none,
But what should go by water. Prithee, tonight
Lay on my bed my wedding sheets: remember;
And call thy husband hither.

I own no one. Don't talk to me, Emilia.
I can't cry and I have no answers
Except for my tears. Please, tonight
Make my bed with the wedding sheets. Do this
And call for my husband.

EMILIA
Here's a change indeed!
Exit

This is a strange change!

DESDEMONA
'Tis meet I should be used so, very meet.
How have I been behaved, that he might stick
The small'st opinion on my least misuse?
Re-enter EMILIA with IAGO

It must be fair for him to treat me like this.
How have I acted that he might complain
About even the smallest problem with me?

IAGO
What is your pleasure, madam?
How is't with you?

What would you like, madam?
How are you?

DESDEMONA
I cannot tell. Those that do teach young babes
Do it with gentle means and easy tasks:
He might have chid me so; for, in good faith,

I am a child to chiding.

I don't know. Parents teach children
Gently, with easy suggestions.
He could have treated me like that, for honestly
I am only a child to being upbraided.

IAGO
What's the matter, lady?

What is the matter, lady?

EMILIA
Alas, Iago, my lord hath so bewhored her.
Thrown such despite and heavy terms upon her,

As true hearts cannot bear.

Iago, Othello has claimed she is a whore.
He has called her such awful names and said such awful things
For hearts to try to bear.

DESDEMONA
Am I that name, Iago?

Am I what he says, Iago?

IAGO
What name, fair lady?

And what is that, fair lady?

DESDEMONA
Such as she says my lord did say I was.

The name she says he called me.

EMILIA
He call'd her whore: a beggar in his drink
Could not have laid such terms upon his callat.

He called her a whore. A poor drunkard
Could not have been so mean to his woman.

IAGO
Why did he so?

Why did he say this?

DESDEMONA
I do not know; I am sure I am none such.

I don't know. I am sure I am not one.

IAGO
Do not weep, do not weep. Alas the day!

Don't cry, don't cry. O awful day!

EMILIA
Hath she forsook so many noble matches,
Her father and her country and her friends,
To be call'd whore? would it not make one weep?

She spurned so many good matches with noble men,
As well as her father, country, and friends,
All to be called a whore? Isn't that enough to make
one cry?

DESDEMONA
It is my wretched fortune.

It is my poor luck.

IAGO
Beshrew him for't!
How comes this trick upon him?

Well curse him for saying it!
How did he get such an idea?

DESDEMONA
Nay, heaven doth know.

Only God knows.

EMILIA
I will be hang'd, if some eternal villain,
Some busy and insinuating rogue,
Some cogging, cozening slave, to get some office,
Have not devised this slander; I'll be hang'd else.

I swear on my life that some villain,
Some meddling and tricky man,
Some lying slave, all for self-gain,
Made up this slanderous falsehood. I swear on my
life.

IAGO
Fie, there is no such man; it is impossible.

No, no such person exists. That's impossible.

DESDEMONA
If any such there be, heaven pardon him!

If there is, may heaven forgive him!

EMILIA
A halter pardon him! and hell gnaw his bones!

A hangman's noose will forgive him! And may hell
have his body!

Why should he call her whore? who keeps her
company?
What place? what time? what form? what
likelihood?
The Moor's abused by some most villanous knave,
Some base notorious knave, some scurvy fellow.
O heaven, that such companions thou'ldst unfold,

Why would he call her a whore? Who spends time
with her?
Where? When? How?

The Moor has been tricked by a villainous enemy,
A notorious criminal, some evil fellow.
O heaven, I wish we could discover who these people
are

And put in every honest hand a whip
To lash the rascals naked through the world
Even from the east to the west!

And give every honest man a whip
So they could beat these rascals everywhere they go,
Across the whole world!

IAGO
Speak within door.

Speak quietly.

EMILIA
O, fie upon them! Some such squire he was
That turn'd your wit the seamy side without,
And made you to suspect me with the Moor.

O curses on them! It;s the same bastard
Who changed your mind to the wrong side
And made you think I slept with the Moor.

IAGO
You are a fool; go to.

You fool, go away.

DESDEMONA
O good Iago,
What shall I do to win my lord again?
Good friend, go to him; for, by this light of heaven,
I know not how I lost him. Here I kneel:
If e'er my will did trespass 'gainst his love,
Either in discourse of thought or actual deed,
Or that mine eyes, mine ears, or any sense,
Delighted them in any other form;
Or that I do not yet, and ever did,
And ever will--though he do shake me off
To beggarly divorcement--love him dearly,

Comfort forswear me! Unkindness may do much;

And his unkindness may defeat my life,
But never taint my love. I cannot say 'whore:'

It does abhor me now I speak the word;
To do the act that might the addition earn
Not the world's mass of vanity could make me.

O Iago,
What can I do to win back Othello?
Good friend, go to him. By the sun above,
I don't know how I lost him. I'm begging you:
If I ever wrong him or his love for me,
Either in what I thought or did,
Or if my eyes, ears, or anything about me
Took pleasure in someone else,
Or that I do not and have not
And never will – even though he might
Divorce me and make me poor – love him
fully,
Than I hope I never have comfort! Being mean
can do a lot,
And his meanness might end my life,
But it will never ruin my love. I cannot say
"whore,"
It disgusts me to even say the word.
To do the act that would gain me that title –
I wouldn't do it for all the fame in the world.

IAGO
I pray you, be content; 'tis but his humour:
The business of the state does him offence,
And he does chide with you.

Please, be happy. This is only a mood,
And the state business is angering him,
He is only taking it out on you.

DESDEMONA
If 'twere no other--

If that's all it is–

IAGO
'Tis but so, I warrant.
Trumpets within
Hark, how these instruments summon to supper!

The messengers of Venice stay the meat;

Go in, and weep not; all things shall be well.

It is, I promise.

Listen! The trumpets are calling out for
dinner.
The messengers from Venice are waiting to
eat.
Go to them, do not cry, and everything will be
alright.

Exeunt DESDEMONA and EMILIA
Enter RODERIGO
How now, Roderigo!

Hello Roderigo!

RODERIGO
I do not find that thou dealest justly with me.

You are not being fair with me.

IAGO
What in the contrary?

Why do you say that?

RODERIGO

Every day thou daffest me with some device, Iago;
and rather, as it seems to me now, keepest from me
all conveniency than suppliest me with the least
advantage of hope. I will indeed no longer endure

it, nor am I yet persuaded to put up in peace what
already I have foolishly suffered.

IAGO

Will you hear me, Roderigo?

RODERIGO

'Faith, I have heard too much, for your words and

performances are no kin together.

IAGO

You charge me most unjustly.

RODERIGO

With nought but truth. I have wasted myself out of

my means. The jewels you have had from me to
deliver to Desdemona would half have corrupted a
votarist: you have told me she hath received them
and returned me expectations and comforts of sudden
respect and acquaintance, but I find none.

IAGO

Well; go to; very well.

RODERIGO

Very well! go to! I cannot go to, man; nor 'tis
not very well: nay, I think it is scurvy, and begin
to find myself fobbed in it.

IAGO

Very well.

RODERIGO

I tell you 'tis not very well. I will make myself

known to Desdemona: if she will return me my

jewels, I will give over my suit and repent my

unlawful solicitation; if not, assure yourself I

will seek satisfaction of you.

---

*Every day you mess with me somehow, Iago,
and now, it seems to me, you keep me from
making any advantage that would give me
the slightest hope. I will not put up with it any
longer
and I am not persuaded to just accept what
I have already suffered.*

Will you hear me out, Roderigo?

*I have already listened to you too much. Your
words
and actions do not fit together.*

You charge me wrongly.

*I charge you only with the truth. I have
exhausted
Everything I have. The jewels that you made
me send to Desdemona would have tempted a
nun. You told me she received them
and would return to me certain comforts
and signs of respect, but I got nothing.*

Fine, go on.

*Fine! Go on! I cannot go on, and it is not
fine. No, it is anything but fine, and I think I
-am being toyed with!*

Fine.

*I am telling you that it is not fine. I will make
sure
that Desdemona knows about me. If she sends
my
jewels back to me, I will give up my case and
apologize
for pursuing her. If she will not send them
back, I
will get my repayment from you.*

IAGO
You have said now.

So you say.

RODERIGO
Ay, and said nothing but what I protest intendment of doing.

Yes, and I say nothing except that which I will do.

IAGO
Why, now I see there's mettle in thee, and even from

this instant to build on thee a better opinion than

ever before. Give me thy hand, Roderigo: thou hast

taken against me a most just exception; but yet, I protest, I have dealt most directly in thy affair.

*Well, I see that there's some fight in you, and from
this moment I am building a better opinion of you
than before. Give me your hand, Roderigo. You have
complained against me very rightly, but still, I have dealt very fairly with you.*

RODERIGO
It hath not appeared.

It doesn't look like it.

IAGO
I grant indeed it hath not appeared, and your suspicion is not without wit and judgment. But, Roderigo, if thou hast that in thee indeed, which I

have greater reason to believe now than ever, I mean purpose, courage and valour, this night show it: if thou the next night following enjoy not Desdemona,

take me from this world with treachery and devise engines for my life.

*I agree, it doesn't look like it, and you
are smart to be suspicious. But,
Roderigo, if you are really a more aggressive person, which I
am beginning to think you are, and have bravery and courage, show it tonight. If tomorrow night you are not sleeping with Desdemona,
than find a way through treachery to take this world away from me.*

RODERIGO
Well, what is it? is it within reason and compass?

Well, what do you want me to do? Is it within my abilities, and is it reasonable?

IAGO
Sir, there is especial commission come from Venice to depute Cassio in Othello's place.

Sir, there has been a special commission from Venice to put Cassio in charge and recall Othello.

RODERIGO
Is that true? why, then Othello and Desdemona return again to Venice.

Really? Than Othello and Desdemona must go back to Venice.

IAGO
O, no; he goes into Mauritania and takes away with him the fair Desdemona, unless his abode be lingered here by some accident: wherein none can be

so determinate as the removing of Cassio.

No, he will go to Mauritania with beautiful Desdemona unless he is kept here through some accidental situation. The best situation for him to stay would be to get rid of Cassio.

RODERIGO

How do you mean, removing of him?

IAGO
Why, by making him uncapable of Othello's place;
knocking out his brains.

RODERIGO
And that you would have me to do?

IAGO
Ay, if you dare do yourself a profit and a right.

He sups to-night with a harlotry, and thither will I
go to him: he knows not yet of his honorable

fortune. If you will watch his going thence, which
I will fashion to fall out between twelve and one,
you may take him at your pleasure: I will be near
to second your attempt, and he shall fall between

us. Come, stand not amazed at it, but go along with

me; I will show you such a necessity in his death
that you shall think yourself bound to put it on
him. It is now high suppertime, and the night grows
to waste: about it.

RODERIGO
I will hear further reason for this.

IAGO
And you shall be satisfied.
Exeunt

What do you mean, "get rid of him"?

*Well, by making him unable to lead –
in other words, to knock out his brains and
kill him.*

And you want me to do that?

*Yes, if you dare do something that will help
you.
He is dining tonight with a prostitute, where I
will meet him. He doesn't know about his
appointment
yet. You must watch when he leaves. I will
make sure he leaves between twelve and one
and then you can snatch him. I will be nearby
to help you, and between the two of us we can
take him.
Come now, stop standing so stunned but come
with
me. I will give you such reasons for his death
that you will find it your obligation to kill
him. It is almost suppertime and we are
wasting time. Let's go.*

I want to hear more about this.

You will hear as much as you want.

Scene III. Another room In the castle.

Enter OTHELLO, LODOVICO, DESDEMONA, EMILIA and Attendants

LODOVICO
I do beseech you, sir, trouble yourself no further.

Please sir, do not trouble yourself anymore.

OTHELLO
O, pardon me: 'twill do me good to walk.

O, excuse me. It would be good for me to take a walk.

LODOVICO
Madam, good night; I humbly thank your ladyship.

Madam, goodnight. I humbly thank you.

DESDEMONA
Your honour is most welcome.

Your welcome.

OTHELLO
Will you walk, sir?
O,--Desdemona,--

Will you walk with me, sir?
O – Desdemona –

DESDEMONA
My lord?

Yes, my lord?

OTHELLO
Get you to bed on the instant; I will be returned
forthwith: dismiss your attendant there: look it be done.

Go to your bed immediately. I will come back soon. Dismiss your attendants as well. Make sure it is done.

DESDEMONA
I will, my lord.
Exeunt OTHELLO, LODOVICO, and Attendants

I will my lord.

EMILIA
How goes it now? he looks gentler than he did.

How is it going? He looks a bit more gentle than he did.

DESDEMONA
He says he will return incontinent:
He hath commanded me to go to bed,
And bade me to dismiss you.

He says he will return shortly
And he commanded me to go to bed
And dismiss you.

EMILIA
Dismiss me!

Dismiss me!

DESDEMONA
It was his bidding: therefore, good Emilia,
Give me my nightly wearing, and adieu:
We must not now displease him.

It was what he asked. So, good Emilia,
Give me my pajamas and good night.
I do not want to upset him now.

EMILIA
I would you had never seen him!

I wish you had never met him!

DESDEMONA
So would not I my love doth so approve him,
That even his stubbornness, his cheques, his frowns--
Prithee, unpin me,--have grace and favour in them.

I don't wish that – I love him regardless,
And even his stubbornness and meanness –
Please, pin this for me – have a beauty to
them.

EMILIA
I have laid those sheets you bade me on the bed.

I put the sheets you asked for on the bed.

DESDEMONA
All's one. Good faith, how foolish are our minds!
If I do die before thee prithee, shroud me
In one of those same sheets.

It doesn't matter. How foolish our minds are!
If I die with you around, please wrap me
In one of these sheets in my coffin.

EMILIA
Come, come you talk.

Come now, don't talk like that.

DESDEMONA
My mother had a maid call'd Barbara:
She was in love, and he she loved proved mad

And did forsake her: she had a song of 'willow;'

An old thing 'twas, but it express'd her fortune,
And she died singing it: that song to-night
Will not go from my mind; I have much to do,
But to go hang my head all at one side,
And sing it like poor Barbara. Prithee, dispatch.

My mother had a maid named Barbara.
She was in love, and the man she loved was
crazy
And left her. She knew a song called
"Willow,"
An old song, but it meant a lot to her
And she died singing it. Tonight that song
Will be in my head. I have a lot to do,
But all the while I hang my head to the side
And sing like Barbara. Please, go now.

EMILIA
Shall I go fetch your night-gown?

Shall I fetch your nightgown?

DESDEMONA
No, unpin me here.
This Lodovico is a proper man.

No, just unpin me here.
Lodovico is a handsome man.

EMILIA
A very handsome man.

Yes, very handsome.

DESDEMONA
He speaks well.

He speaks well, also.

EMILIA
I know a lady in Venice would have walked barefoot

to Palestine for a touch of his nether lip.

I know a lady from Venice who would have
walked barefoot
all the way to Palestine just to kiss his lip.

DESDEMONA
[Singing]The poor soul sat sighing by a sycamore tree,

Sing all a green willow:
Her hand on her bosom, her head on her knee,

The poor woman sat crying by the sycamore
tree,
Everyone sing with the willow:
Her hand on her chest, her head on her knee,

Sing willow, willow, willow:
The fresh streams ran by her, and murmur'd her moans;

Sing willow, willow, willow;
Her salt tears fell from her, and soften'd the stones;
Lay by these:--

Singing
Sing willow, willow, willow;
Prithee, hie thee; he'll come anon:--
Singing
Sing all a green willow must be my garland.

Let nobody blame him; his scorn I approve,-

Nay, that's not next.--Hark! who is't that knocks?

EMILIA
It's the wind.

DESDEMONA
[Singing] I call'd my love false love; but what
said he then?
Sing willow, willow, willow:
If I court moe women, you'll couch with moe men!

So, get thee gone; good night, Mine eyes do itch;
Doth that bode weeping?

EMILIA
'Tis neither here nor there.

DESDEMONA
I have heard it said so. O, these men, these men!

Dost thou in conscience think,--tell me, Emilia,--

That there be women do abuse their husbands
In such gross kind?

EMILIA
There be some such, no question.

DESDEMONA
Wouldst thou do such a deed for all the world?

EMILIA
Why, would not you?

DESDEMONA
No, by this heavenly light!

Sing willow, willow, willow:
The fresh streams ran past her and
murmured like she did,
Sing willow, willow, willow:
Her tears fell and softened the stones–
Put them here –

Sing willow, willow, willow–
Please, get going, he will come soon –

Everyone sing with the willow, a
willow my necklace,
Let nobody blame him for he is right to
hate me–
No, that doesn't come next – Listen!
Who is knocking?

It's only the wind.

I told me lover he didn't really love me
but what did he say?
Sing willow, willow, willow:
If I chase more women, you will sleep
with more men!
So get going, goodnight. My eyes itch–
Does that mean I will soon start
crying?

It doesn't mean anything.

I have heard something about it
before. O, these men!
Do you honestly think – be true,
Emilia –
That women hurt their husbands
Just as much?

Some do, undoubtedly.

Would you ever do such a thing for all
the money in the world?

Why, would you?

No, I swear by heaven!

EMILIA
Nor I neither by this heavenly light;
I might do't as well i' the dark.

Well I wouldn't by heaven's light either,
But I might in the dark.

DESDEMONA
Wouldst thou do such a deed for all the world?

Is there anything in the world that could make
you do it?

EMILIA
The world's a huge thing: it is a great price.
For a small vice.

The world is a big, expensive thing
For a small sin.

DESDEMONA
In troth, I think thou wouldst not.

Truly, I don't think you would do it.

EMILIA
In troth, I think I should; and undo't when I had

done. Marry, I would not do such a thing for a
joint-ring, nor for measures of lawn, nor for
gowns, petticoats, nor caps, nor any petty
exhibition; but for the whole world,--why, who would

not make her husband a cuckold to make him a

monarch? I should venture purgatory for't.

Actually, I might do it, and then undo it when
it was
done. I wouldn't do such a thing for
a ring or for a garden, not for
dresses or petticoats or caps or any small
thing, but for the wholed world... why, would
wouldn't
cheat on her husband if afterwards she could
make him
a king? I would risk purgatory for it.

DESDEMONA
Beshrew me, if I would do such a wrong
For the whole world.

Curse me if I would do such a thing,
Even for the whole world.

EMILIA
Why the wrong is but a wrong i' the world: and

having the world for your labour, tis a wrong in your

own world, and you might quickly make it right.

Well it is only wrong insofar as it is in the
world, and
if your wrong ends up winning you the whole
world, than it is wrong
in your world – you might as well make it
right, then.

DESDEMONA
I do not think there is any such woman.

I don't think such a woman exists.

EMILIA
Yes, a dozen; and as many to the vantage as would

Store the world they played for.
But I do think it is their husbands' faults
If wives do fall: say that they slack their duties,

And pour our treasures into foreign laps,
Or else break out in peevish jealousies,

They do, dozens of them, as many as would
exist
In the world they did it for.
But I do think it is the husbands' faults
If wives cheat on them. Say that the husbands
stop their duties to us as their wives
And instead sleep with other women,
Or say they become annoyingly jealous,

Throwing restraint upon us; or say they strike us,

Or scant our former having in despite;
Why, we have galls, and though we have some grace,

Yet have we some revenge. Let husbands know

Their wives have sense like them: they see and smell

And have their palates both for sweet and sour,
As husbands have. What is it that they do
When they change us for others? Is it sport?
I think it is: and doth affection breed it?
I think it doth: is't frailty that thus errs?

It is so too: and have not we affections,
Desires for sport, and frailty, as men have?

Then let them use us well: else let them know,

The ills we do, their ills instruct us so.

DESDEMONA
Good night, good night: heaven me such uses send,

Not to pick bad from bad, but by bad mend!

Exeunt

And make us stick to rules they impose, or say they hit us
Or stop letting us have access to money –
Well, we have backbones, and even though we might be gracious,
We can take our revenge. Husbands should know
That their wives are like them: they see and smell
And have tastes for sweet and sour
Just like their husbands. Why do they
Exchange us for other women? For fun?
I think so. For lust and affection?
That too. Is it their weaknesses that makes them fall?
Yes, that too: but don't we have lust as well,
And desire for fun, and weaknesses, just like men do?
Then we should use them also, or else we should let them know
That if we do something wrong, it is because they do.

Goodnight, goodnight. I pray God will help me use this information
Not so that I learn from the bad, but so that I can avoid becoming like that!

Act V

Scene I. Cyprus. A street.

Enter IAGO and RODERIGO

IAGO
Here, stand behind this bulk; straight will he come:

Wear thy good rapier bare, and put it home:

Quick, quick; fear nothing; I'll be at thy elbow:

It makes us, or it mars us; think on that,

And fix most firm thy resolution.

Stand here behind the wall and he will come here soon.
Keep your sword unsheathed, and then drive it in him.
Do it quickly and do not fear, I will be beside you.
This will help us or it will hurt us, so think about that
And carry through with determination.

RODERIGO
Be near at hand; I may miscarry in't.

Be close, I may miss him.

IAGO
Here, at thy hand: be bold, and take thy stand.
Retires

Here, stay close. Be bold and take a stand.

RODERIGO
I have no great devotion to the deed;
And yet he hath given me satisfying reasons:
'Tis but a man gone. Forth, my sword: he dies.

I don't really want to do this,
But he gave me strong reasons.
One man gone. First my sword in him, and then he dies.

IAGO
I have rubb'd this young quat almost to the sense,

And he grows angry. Now, whether he kill Cassio,

Or Cassio him, or each do kill the other,
Every way makes my gain: live Roderigo,

He calls me to a restitution large
Of gold and jewels that I bobb'd from him,
As gifts to Desdemona;
It must not be: if Cassio do remain,
He hath a daily beauty in his life
That makes me ugly; and, besides, the Moor

May unfold me to him; there stand I in much peril:

No, he must die. But so: I hear him coming.
Enter CASSIO

I have inflamed this pimple until it is ready to pop,
And he is getting angry. Now. whether he kills Cassio
Or Cassio kills him, or they kill each other–
Every combination can work for me. But if Roderigo lives,
Then he will ask me to repay him
For the gold and jewels I stole from him
As if they were gifts to Desdemona.
That shouldn't happen. If Cassio remains,
Then his natural handsomeness
Makes me comparatively look ugly. And besides, the Moor
Might talk to him about what I have been telling him. That would be dangerous for me.
No, he must die as well. I hear him coming.

RODERIGO
I know his gait, 'tis he.--Villain, thou diest!
Makes a pass at CASSIO

I know those steps, it's Cassio. –Villain! Die!

CASSIO
That thrust had been mine enemy indeed,
But that my coat is better than thou know'st
I will make proof of thine.

Draws, and wounds RODERIGO

RODERIGO
O, I am slain!
IAGO from behind wounds CASSIO in the leg, and exit

CASSIO
I am maim'd for ever. Help, ho! murder! murder!
Falls
Enter OTHELLO

OTHELLO
The voice of Cassio: Iago keeps his word.

RODERIGO
O, villain that I am!

OTHELLO
It is even so.

CASSIO
O, help, ho! light! a surgeon!

OTHELLO
'Tis he:--O brave Iago, honest and just,
That hast such noble sense of thy friend's wrong!

Thou teachest me. Minion, your dear lies dead,

And your unblest fate hies: strumpet, I come.
Forth of my heart those charms, thine eyes, are blotted;
Thy bed, lust-stain'd, shall with lust's blood be spotted.

Exit
Enter LODOVICO and GRATIANO

CASSIO
What, ho! no watch? no passage? murder! murder!

GRATIANO
'Tis some mischance; the cry is very direful.

CASSIO
O, help!

That is the thrust of an enemy,
But I have armor underneath my coat,
And now we will see how strong your clothing is.

O, I am dead!

I am injured forever! Help! Murder! Murder!

That's the voice of Cassio. Iago has kept his word.

O I am such a villain!

That's true.

O, help! Get a light! Get a surgeon!

It's he. O brave Iago, honest and just,
You have such a noble understanding of your friend's hurt!

You teach me well. Whore, here, dead, is your lover,
And your fate is coming soon.
Your eyes have been shut out of my heart.
You stained the bed with lust, now your lusting blood will stain it.

What! No guard? No one here? Murder!

Something is wrong – that cry sounds very bad.

Help!

LODOVICO
Hark!

Listen!

RODERIGO
O wretched villain!

O evil man!

LODOVICO
Two or three groan: it is a heavy night:

These may be counterfeits: let's think't unsafe
To come in to the cry without more help.

Two or three are groaning there. It is a dark night,
These might be fake. It might be unsafe
To go to the cry without more help with us.

RODERIGO
Nobody come? then shall I bleed to death.

Nobody is coming? I will bleed to death!

LODOVICO
Hark!
Re-enter IAGO, with a light

Listen!

GRATIANO
Here's one comes in his shirt, with light and weapons.

Here comes someone with no coat on, with a light and with weapons.

IAGO
Who's there? whose noise is this that ones on murder?

Who is htere? Who is shouting "murder"?

LODOVICO
We do not know.

We don't know.

IAGO
Did not you hear a cry?

Did you hear the cries?

CASSIO
Here, here! for heaven's sake, help me!

Here, here, help me!

IAGO
What's the matter?

What is the matter?

GRATIANO
This is Othello's ancient, as I take it.

That is Othello's ensign, I think

LODOVICO
The same indeed; a very valiant fellow.

It is, and he is a good man.

IAGO
What are you here that cry so grievously?

Who is crying so loudly here?

CASSIO
Iago? O, I am spoil'd, undone by villains!
Give me some help.

Iago? O I am hurt, destroyed by criminals!
Get me help!

IAGO
O me, lieutenant! what villains have done this?

O, lieutenant! What criminals have done this?

CASSIO
I think that one of them is hereabout,
And cannot make away.

I think one is nearby,
And can't get away.

IAGO
O treacherous villains!
What are you there? come in, and give some help.

O evil men!
Why are you standing there? Come in and
help.

To LODOVICO and GRATIANO

RODERIGO
O, help me here!

O help me here!

CASSIO
That's one of them.

That must be one of them.

IAGO
O murderous slave! O villain!
Stabs RODERIGO

Murderer! Villain!

RODERIGO
O damn'd Iago! O inhuman dog!

O damn you Iago, you inhuman dog!

IAGO
Kill men i' the dark!--Where be these bloody thieves?--

How silent is this town!--Ho! murder! murder!--

What may you be? are you of good or evil?

How awful to kill men in the dark! – Where
are the other thieves? –
And this is such a quiet town! – Murder!
murder!–
Who is coming? Friend or foe?

LODOVICO
As you shall prove us, praise us.

Judge us and see we are friends.

IAGO
Signior Lodovico?

Sir Lodovico?

LODOVICO
He, sir.

I am he, sir.

IAGO
I cry you mercy. Here's Cassio hurt by villains.

I beg you for mercy. Cassio is here, injured by
criminals.

GRATIANO
Cassio!

Cassio!

IAGO
How is't, brother!

How did this happen! My brother!

CASSIO
My leg is cut in two.

My leg is sliced into two.

IAGO
Marry, heaven forbid!
Light, gentlemen; I'll bind it with my shirt.

O, God forbid!
Bring the light, gentlemen. I will cover the wound with my shirt.

Enter BIANCA

BIANCA
What is the matter, ho? who is't that cried?

What is the matter? Who is crying out?

IAGO
Who is't that cried!

Who has cried!

BIANCA
O my dear Cassio! my sweet Cassio! O Cassio, Cassio, Cassio!

O my dear Cassio! Cassio! O Cassio, Cassio, Cassio!

IAGO
O notable strumpet! Cassio, may you suspect

Who they should be that have thus many led you?

Notorious prostitute! Cassio, do you know
Who attacked you?

CASSIO
No.

No.

GRATIANO
I am to find you thus: I have been to seek you.

I am sorry to see you like this, I have been trying to find you.

IAGO
Lend me a garter. So. O, for a chair,

To bear him easily hence!

Give me your sash. O, if only we had a chair
To carry him away on.

BIANCA
Alas, he faints! O Cassio, Cassio, Cassio!

No, he is fainting! O Cassio, Cassio, Cassio!

IAGO
Gentlemen all, I do suspect this trash
To be a party in this injury.
Patience awhile, good Cassio. Come, come;
Lend me a light. Know we this face or no?

Alas my friend and my dear countryman
Roderigo! no:--yes, sure: O heaven! Roderigo.

Gentlemen, I think that this trashy girl
Is part of this situation.
Be patient, good Cassio. Come, come,
Put a light on this. Does anyone recognize this face?
O, it is my friend and countryman
Roderigo! It can't be – yes, it is, oh no! Roderigo.

GRATIANO
What, of Venice?

From Venice?

IAGO
Even he, sir; did you know him?

That's him, sir – did you know him?

GRATIANO
Know him! ay.

Know him! Yes.

IAGO
Signior Gratiano? I cry you gentle pardon;
These bloody accidents must excuse my manners,

That so neglected you.

Sir Gratiano? I ask for your pardon.
These bloody events have made me forget my manners,
And I ignored you.

GRATIANO
I am glad to see you.

I am glad to see you.

IAGO
How do you, Cassio? O, a chair, a chair!

Cassio, are you alright? Bring a chair!

GRATIANO
Roderigo!

Roderigo!

IAGO
He, he 'tis he.
A chair brought in
O, that's well said; the chair!

Yes, it's him.

O, good, the chair!

GRATIANO
Some good man bear him carefully from hence;
I'll fetch the general's surgeon.
To BIANCA
For you, mistress,
Save you your labour. He that lies slain here, Cassio,
Was my dear friend: what malice was between you?

Some strong men need to carry him carefully.
I will get the general's surgeon.

As for you, mistress,
Calm down. Cassio, the man who is dead here
Was a friend of mine. What argument was
between you?

CASSIO
None in the world; nor do I know the man.

None in the world: I don't even know him.

IAGO
[To BIANCA] What, look you pale?
O, bear him out o' the air.
CASSIO and RODERIGO are borne off
Stay you, good gentlemen. Look you pale, mistress?

Do you perceive the gastness of her eye?
Nay, if you stare, we shall hear more anon.
Behold her well; I pray you, look upon her:
Do you see, gentlemen? nay, guiltiness will speak,
Though tongues were out of use.
Enter EMILIA

Why do you look so pale?
O carry him away.

Stay and look, good gentlemen. Are you pale,
mistress?
Do you all see how afraid she looks?
If you watch her, we will hear more soon.
Watch her well, please, watch her well:
Do you see, men? Her guiltiness will speak
Even if she is silent.

EMILIA
'Las, what's the matter? what's the matter, husband?

Oh no, what is the matter? Husband, what is the matter?

IAGO
Cassio hath here been set on in the dark
By Roderigo and fellows that are scaped:
He's almost slain, and Roderigo dead.

*Cassio has been attached in the dark
By Roderigo and others who escaped.
He is hurt badly, and Roderigo is dead.*

EMILIA
Alas, good gentleman! alas, good Cassio!

O my! Good gentlemen! O no, good Cassio!

IAGO
This is the fruit of whoring. Prithee, Emilia,

Go know of Cassio where he supp'd to-night.
To BIANCA
What, do you shake at that?

*This is what happens when you visit whores.
Please, Emilia,
Go find out where Cassio had dinner tonight.*

Why are you shaking?

BIANCA
He supp'd at my house; but I therefore shake not.

He ate at my house, but I am not shaking.

IAGO
O, did he so? I charge you, go with me.

O he did? You must come with me.

EMILIA
Fie, fie upon thee, strumpet!

Curses on you, whore!

BIANCA
I am no strumpet; but of life as honest
As you that thus abuse me.

*I am no whore. I am as honest
As all of you who curse me.*

EMILIA
As I! foh! fie upon thee!

As me! No! Curses on you!

IAGO
Kind gentlemen, let's go see poor Cassio dress'd.

Come, mistress, you must tell's another tale.
Emilia run you to the citadel,
And tell my lord and lady what hath happ'd.
Will you go on? I pray.
Aside
This is the night
That either makes me or fordoes me quite.
Exeunt

*Gentlemen, let us visit Cassio as he is tended to.
Come mistress, you must tell your story.
Emilia, run to the castle
And tell my lord and lady what happened.
Will you go now? Please.*

*Tonight
Either makes my fortunes or ruins me.*

Scene II. A bedchamber in the castle: DESDEMONA in bed asleep; a light burning.

Enter OTHELLO

OTHELLO
It is the cause, it is the cause, my soul,--
Let me not name it to you, you chaste stars!--
It is the cause. Yet I'll not shed her blood;
Nor scar that whiter skin of hers than snow,

And smooth as monumental alabaster.
Yet she must die, else she'll betray more men.

Put out the light, and then put out the light:

If I quench thee, thou flaming minister,
I can again thy former light restore,
Should I repent me: but once put out thy light,

Thou cunning'st pattern of excelling nature,
I know not where is that Promethean heat
That can thy light relume. When I have pluck'd the rose,

I cannot give it vital growth again.
It must needs wither: I'll smell it on the tree.

Kissing her
Ah balmy breath, that dost almost persuade
Justice to break her sword! One more, one more.

Be thus when thou art dead, and I will kill thee,

And love thee after. One more, and this the last:

So sweet was ne'er so fatal. I must weep,

But they are cruel tears: this sorrow's heavenly;

It strikes where it doth love. She wakes.

DESDEMONA
Who's there? Othello?

OTHELLO
Ay. Desdemona.

DESDEMONA
Will you come to bed, my lord?

I have good reason, I have good reason –
I won't say it to you, O pure stars! –
I have good reason. I won't make her bleed
Nor will I scar her skin that is as white as snow,
And as smooth as alabaster stone.
Yet if she doesn't die she will betray even more men.
I will put out the light of the candle, and then the light of her life.
If I put you out, you flaming candle,
I can always light you again
If I feel sorry for it. But once I put out Desdemona's light,
That beautiful, cunning woman,
Then I do not know what heat
Can relit her life. When I have picked that rose,
I cannot give it life again.
It must wither. I will smell it once more while it is alive on the tree.

Sweet breath, you almost persuade me
Not to kill you and not to carry out the deserved justice. One more kiss.
If you look like this when you are dead, then I will kill you
And I will love you afterwards. One more kiss, and this is the last one.
Something so sweet was never so fatal. I must cry,
But I must be cruel as well. This is a Godly sorrow
Which punishes the one it loves. She is waking up.

Who is there? Othello?

Yes, Desdemona.

Will you please come to bed, my lord?

OTHELLO
Have you pray'd to-night, Desdemona?

Have you prayed tonight, Desdemona?

DESDEMONA
Ay, my lord.

yes, my lord.

OTHELLO
If you bethink yourself of any crime
Unreconciled as yet to heaven and grace,
Solicit for it straight.

*If you can think of any crime
That you have not asked for forgiveness for,
Do that now.*

DESDEMONA
Alas, my lord, what do you mean by that?

My lord, what do you mean?

OTHELLO
Well, do it, and be brief; I will walk by:
I would not kill thy unprepared spirit;

No; heaven forfend! I would not kill thy soul.

*Do it, and be quick. I will wait,
For I will not kill someone who is not
spiritually ready.
No, by God I would not want your soul to go
to hell.*

DESDEMONA
Talk you of killing?

You are talking about killing?

OTHELLO
Ay, I do.

I am.

DESDEMONA
Then heaven
Have mercy on me!

*God
Have mercy on me!*

OTHELLO
Amen, with all my heart!

Amen to that!

DESDEMONA
If you say so, I hope you will not kill me.

Since you say so, I hope you will not kill me.

OTHELLO
Hum!

Hmm!

DESDEMONA
And yet I fear you; for you are fatal then

When your eyes roll so: why I should fear I know not,

Since guiltiness I know not; but yet I feel I fear.

*Yet I am afraid of you, for you are deadly and
dangerous
When your eyes are so red. I don't know why I
am afraid,
Since I am not guilty of anything, but I still
feel fear.*

OTHELLO
Think on thy sins.

Think about your sins.

DESDEMONA
They are loves I bear to you.

The only one is the love I have for you.

OTHELLO
Ay, and for that thou diest.

And that is why you will die.

DESDEMONA
That death's unnatural that kills for loving.
Alas, why gnaw you so your nether lip?
Some bloody passion shakes your very frame:
These are portents; but yet I hope, I hope,
They do not point on me.

It isn't right to kill someone for loving.
O, why are you biting your lip?
A strong, evil emotion is shaking your body.
This is some bad omen, but still I hope
That it does not bode poorly for me.

OTHELLO
Peace, and be still!

Be quiet and still!

DESDEMONA
I will so. What's the matter?

I will. What is the matter?

OTHELLO
That handkerchief which I so loved and gave thee
Thou gavest to Cassio.

The handkerchief that I loved and gave to you,
You gave to Cassio.

DESDEMONA
No, by my life and soul!
Send for the man, and ask him.

I didn't, I swear by my life and soul!
Send for him and ask him.

OTHELLO
Sweet soul, take heed,
Take heed of perjury; thou art on thy deathbed.

Sweet soul, be careful,
Be careful not to lie, for you are on your
deathbed.

DESDEMONA
Ay, but not yet to die.

Yes, but I have not died yet.

OTHELLO
Yes, presently:
Therefore confess thee freely of thy sin;
For to deny each article with oath

Cannot remove nor choke the strong conception
That I do groan withal. Thou art to die.

Soon,
So confess your sin openly:
It won't help you to swear against each
accusation,
That won't remove the thought that makes me
Groan in pain. You are going to die.

DESDEMONA
Then Lord have mercy on me!

Lord have mercy on me!

OTHELLO
I say, amen.

Again, I say Amen.

DESDEMONA
And have you mercy too! I never did

And you have mercy on me too! I never did
anything

Offend you in my life; never loved Cassio
But with such general warranty of heaven

As I might love: I never gave him token.

OTHELLO
By heaven, I saw my handkerchief in's hand.
O perjured woman! thou dost stone my heart,
And makest me call what I intend to do
A murder, which I thought a sacrifice:
I saw the handkerchief.

DESDEMONA
He found it then;
I never gave it him: send for him hither;
Let him confess a truth.

OTHELLO
He hath confess'd.

DESDEMONA
What, my lord?

OTHELLO
That he hath used thee.

DESDEMONA
How? unlawfully?

OTHELLO
Ay.

DESDEMONA
He will not say so.

OTHELLO
No, his mouth is stopp'd;
Honest Iago hath ta'en order for't.

DESDEMONA
O! my fear interprets: what, is he dead?

OTHELLO
Had all his hairs been lives, my great revenge

Had stomach for them all.

DESDEMONA
Alas! he is betray'd and I undone.

*To offend you. I never loved Cassio
Except with the rule of heaven that towards anyone
I could love. I never gave him that handkerchief.*

*By God, I saw it in his hand,
You lying woman! You turn my heart to stone,
And make me call what I am about to do
A murder, when I thought it was a sacrifice.
I saw the handkerchief.*

*He must have found it then.
I never gave it to him. Send for him,
And let him confess the truth.*

He already confessed.

What, my lord?

That he had sex with you.

What? That he had sex with me?

Yes.

He will not say that.

*No, not now. His mouth won't say anything
Since honest Iago has taken care of him.*

O no! I am afraid to interpret that. Is he dead?

*If he had as many lives as he had hairs, I would have had
A desire to take revenge on all of them.*

No! Someone has betrayed him, and I am ruined.

OTHELLO
Out, strumpet! weep'st thou for him to my face?

You whore! You dare cry over him in front of me.

DESDEMONA
O, banish me, my lord, but kill me not!

My lord, banish me but do not kill me!

OTHELLO
Down, strumpet!

Sit down, whore!

DESDEMONA
Kill me to-morrow: let me live to-night!

Kill me tomorrow, but let me live tonight!

OTHELLO
Nay, if you strive--

No, if you struggle–

DESDEMONA
But half an hour!

Just half an hour more!

OTHELLO
Being done, there is no pause.

There is no sense in pausing now.

DESDEMONA
But while I say one prayer!

Let me say one prayer!

OTHELLO
It is too late.
He stifles her

It is too late.

EMILIA
[Within] My lord , my lord! what, ho! my lord, my lord!

My lord, my lord! What! Hello! My lord!

OTHELLO
What noise is this? Not dead? not yet quite dead?
I that am cruel am yet merciful;
I would not have thee linger in thy pain: So, so.

What noise is this? Are you not dead yet? Yet?
I might be cruel, but I am still merciful enough
That I would not want you to be in pain.

EMILIA
[Within] What, ho! my lord, my lord!

What! My lord! My lord!

OTHELLO
Who's there?

Who is it?

EMILIA
[Within] O, good my lord, I would speak a word with you!

O my lord, I must tell you something!

OTHELLO
Yes: 'tis Emilia. By and by. She's dead.
'Tis like she comes to speak of Cassio's death.--

It is Emilia. I'm coming. Ok, she's dead.
She is likely coming here to tell me about
Cassio's death.–

The noise was here. Ha! no more moving?

Still as the grave. Shall she come in? were't good?—

I think she stirs again:--no. What's best to do?

If she come in, she'll sure speak to my wife:

My wife! my wife! what wife? I have no wife.
O insupportable! O heavy hour!
Methinks it should be now a huge eclipse
Of sun and moon, and that the affrighted globe
Should yawn at alteration.

EMILIA
[Within] I do beseech you
That I may speak with you, O, good my lord!

OTHELLO
I had forgot thee: O, come in, Emilia;
Soft; by and by. Let me the curtains draw.
Where art thou?
Unlocks the door
What's the matter with thee now?

EMILIA
O, my good lord, yonder's foul murders done!

OTHELLO
What, now?

EMILIA
But now, my lord.

OTHELLO
It is the very error of the moon;
She comes more nearer earth than she was wont,

And makes men mad.

EMILIA
Cassio, my lord, hath kill'd a young Venetian
Call'd Roderigo.

OTHELLO
Roderigo kill'd!
And Cassio kill'd!

EMILIA
No, Cassio is not kill'd.

The noise of the fight was near here. Now! No more moving?
She is as still as a grave. Should Emilia come in? Is that a good idea?–
I think she is moving again. No. What should I do?
If she comes in, she will want to speak to my wife:
My wife! my wife! what wife? I have no wife.
O this is an unbearable and sad time!
I would have guessed that a huge eclipse
Of the sun and the moon would have occurred
Now that Desdemona is off of the planet.

Please,
I must speak to you, my lord!

I forgot about you, come in Emilia.
Wait and let me draw the curtains.
Where are you?
Enter EMILIA
Now what's the matter?

My lord, awful murders have occurred!

What, just now?

Just now, my lord.

It must be because of the moon:
It has come closer to the earth than it usually does,
And it drives men crazy.

My lord, Cassio has killed a young Venetian
Named Roderigo.

Roderigo dead!
And Cassio dead!

No, Cassio is not yet dead.

OTHELLO
Not Cassio kill'd! then murder's out of tune,

And sweet revenge grows harsh.

Cassio is not dead? Then the murder is wrong,
And my revenge is ruined.

DESDEMONA
O, falsely, falsely murder'd!

O I have been wrongly murdered!

EMILIA
Alas, what cry is that?

O what is that cry!

OTHELLO
That! what?

What? That?

EMILIA
Out, and alas! that was my lady's voice.
Help! help, ho! help! O lady, speak again!
Sweet Desdemona! O sweet mistress, speak!

Oh no! It was my lady's voice!
Help! Help! Help! O lady, speak again!
Sweet Desdemona! My mistress speak!

DESDEMONA
A guiltless death I die.

I die without blame.

EMILIA
O, who hath done this deed?

Who has done this to you?

DESDEMONA
Nobody; I myself. Farewell
Commend me to my kind lord: O, farewell!
Dies

Nobody, I did it to myself. Goodbye
And give my love to my lord. Goodbye!

OTHELLO
Why, how should she be murder'd?

How was she murdered?

EMILIA
Alas, who knows?

Who knows?

OTHELLO
You heard her say herself, it was not I.

You heard her say it was not me.

EMILIA
She said so: I must needs report the truth.

Yes, that's what she said. I must report this.

OTHELLO
She's, like a liar, gone to burning hell:
'Twas I that kill'd her.

She lied even as she was going to hell.
It was me. I killed her.

EMILIA
O, the more angel she,
And you the blacker devil!

O then she is an angel for it
And you are a devil for it!

OTHELLO
She turn'd to folly, and she was a whore.

She cheated on me and became a whore.

EMILIA
Thou dost belie her, and thou art a devil.

You are lying about her. You are a devil.

OTHELLO
She was false as water.

She was as unfaithful as water.

EMILIA
Thou art rash as fire, to say
That she was false: O, she was heavenly true!

*You are mean and angry like fire if you
Think she was unfaithful. She was purely true
to you!*

OTHELLO
Cassio did top her; ask thy husband else.
O, I were damn'd beneath all depth in hell,
But that I did proceed upon just grounds

To this extremity. Thy husband knew it all.

*Cassio had sex with her, ask your husband.
I would damn myself to the depths of hell
If I did not do what I did from certain grounds
of proof.
Your husband knew everything.*

EMILIA
My husband!

My husband!

OTHELLO
Thy husband.

Your husband.

EMILIA
That she was false to wedlock?

He said she was unfaithful?

OTHELLO
Ay, with Cassio. Nay, had she been true,
If heaven would make me such another world
Of one entire and Perfect chrysolite,
I'ld not have sold her for it.

*Yes, with Cassio. If she had remained faithful,
Heaven could have created another world
Of perfect crystal
And I would not have sold her for it.*

EMILIA
My husband!

My husband!

OTHELLO
Ay, 'twas he that told me first:
An honest man he is, and hates the slime
That sticks on filthy deeds.

*Yes, he told me about it first.
He is an honest man and hates the effects
Of evil actions.*

EMILIA
My husband!

My husband!

OTHELLO
What needs this iteration, woman? I say thy husband.

*Why do you keep repeating this, woman? Yes,
your husband.*

EMILIA
O mistress, villany hath made mocks with love,
My husband say that she was false!

*O my lady. a villain has mocked your love.
My husband said that she was unfaithful!*

OTHELLO
He, woman;
I say thy husband: dost understand the word?

My friend, thy husband, honest, honest Iago.

Yes, woman,
Your husband. Do you understand that word,
"husband"?
My friend, your husband, the honest Iago.

EMILIA
If he say so, may his pernicious soul
Rot half a grain a day! he lies to the heart:
She was too fond of her most filthy bargain.

If he said that, then his evil soul
Should rot in hell! He is lying completely.
She loved her awful marriage to you.

OTHELLO
Ha!

Ha!

EMILIA
Do thy worst:
This deed of thine is no more worthy heaven
Than thou wast worthy her.

Do your worst.
You can kill me and it will not get you into heaven,
Just like you weren't worthy of her to begin with.

OTHELLO
Peace, you were best.

You would be best if you shut up.

EMILIA
Thou hast not half that power to do me harm
As I have to be hurt. O gull! O dolt!
As ignorant as dirt! thou hast done a deed--
I care not for thy sword; I'll make thee known,

Though I lost twenty lives.--Help! help, ho! help!
The Moor hath kill'd my mistress! Murder!
murder!
Enter MONTANO, GRATIANO, IAGO, and others

You can't hurt me, I can endure much more
Than you can do to me. You fool!
As dumb as dirt! You have done an awful thing–
I do not care about your sword. I'll make sure others
know what you did
Even if I lost my life twenty times. – Help! help! help!
The Moor killed my lady! Murder! murder!

MONTANO
What is the matter? How now, general!

What is the matter? What is going on, general?

EMILIA
O, are you come, Iago? you have done well,
That men must lay their murders on your neck.

O have you come too, Iago? You have done very well,
Since men are claiming you are the reason for
murdering others.

GRATIANO
What is the matter?

What is going on?

EMILIA
Disprove this villain, if thou be'st a man:
He says thou told'st him that his wife was false:
I know thou didst not, thou'rt not such a villain:

Speak, for my heart is full.

Tell this criminal that he is wrong, if you are a man.
He says that you told him his wife was unfaithful,
And I know that you did not. You can't be such a
criminal.
Speak, I am too full of emotion.

IAGO
I told him what I thought, and told no more
Than what he found himself was apt and true.

I told him what I thought, and nothing else.
He found the proof and truth behind the rest
of it.

EMILIA
But did you ever tell him she was false?

But did you tell him she was unfaithful?

IAGO
I did.

I did.

EMILIA
You told a lie, an odious, damned lie;
Upon my soul, a lie, a wicked lie.
She false with Cassio!--did you say with Cassio?

Then you lied, an awful, cursed lie.
On my soul, a wicked lie.
She unfaithful with Cassio! Is that what you
said?

IAGO
With Cassio, mistress. Go to, charm your tongue.

With Cassio, mistress. Now hold your tongue
and be quiet.

EMILIA
I will not charm my tongue; I am bound to speak:
My mistress here lies murder'd in her bed,--

I will not be quiet, I must speak.
My lady has been murdered in her bed–

All
O heavens forfend!

God forbid!

EMILIA
And your reports have set the murder on.

And your lies led to the murder.

OTHELLO
Nay, stare not, masters: it is true, indeed.

Stop staring, sirs. It's true.

GRATIANO
'Tis a strange truth.

This is unbelievable.

MONTANO
O monstrous act!

A horrifying act!

EMILIA
Villany, villany, villany!
I think upon't, I think: I smell't: O villany!--

I thought so then:--I'll kill myself for grief:--

O villany, villany!

Evil, evil, evil!
I can't stop thinking about it. I even smell the
evil!
I suspected as much – I will kill myself for
sorrow–
O evil!

IAGO
What, are you mad? I charge you, get you home.

Have you gone mad? I order you, go home.

EMILIA
Good gentlemen, let me have leave to speak:

Good men, give me permission to speak.

'Tis proper I obey him, but not now.

Perchance, Iago, I will ne'er go home.

OTHELLO
O! O! O!
He falls on the bed

EMILIA
Nay, lay thee down and roar;
For thou hast kill'd the sweetest innocent

That e'er did lift up eye.

OTHELLO
[Rising] O, she was foul!
I scarce did know you, uncle: there lies your niece,

Whose breath, indeed, these hands have newly stopp'd:

I know this act shows horrible and grim.

GRATIANO
Poor Desdemona! I am glad thy father's dead:

Thy match was mortal to him, and pure grief

Shore his old thread in twain: did he live now,
This sight would make him do a desperate turn,

Yea, curse his better angel from his side,
And fall to reprobation.

OTHELLO
'Tis pitiful; but yet Iago knows
That she with Cassio hath the act of shame
A thousand times committed; Cassio confess'd it:
And she did gratify his amorous works
With that recognizance and pledge of love
Which I first gave her; I saw it in his hand:
It was a handkerchief, an antique token
My father gave my mother.

EMILIA
O heaven! O heavenly powers!

IAGO-
Come, hold your peace.

EMILIA
'Twill out, 'twill out: I peace!

It is usually appropriate to obey him, but not now.
Maybe, Iago, I will never go home to you.

O, O, O!

Go ahead and lay down and moan,
For you have killed the most beautiful and innocent woman
Who ever lived.

She was evil!
I barely knew you, Uncle Gratiano, but there is your niece,
Whose breath I have recently stopped by choking her.
I know this sounds horrible.

Poor Desdemona! I am glad your father is dead:
The marriage was too much for him and from his sadness
He died before his time. If he were alive now,
Seeing this would cause him to do desperate things.
Yes, he would even curse his goodness
And end up in hell.

This is sad, but Iago knows
That she and Cassio have slept together
A thousand times. Cassio confessed to it.
And she returned her favor to his love
With a pledge of her own love by giving him
What I first gave to her. I saw it in his hand:
It was my handkerchief, an old token
That my father game to my mother.

O heaven! O God!

Stop, be quiet.

The truth will come out! Me keep quiet?

No, I will speak as liberal as the north:
Let heaven and men and devils, let them all,
All, all, cry shame against me, yet I'll speak.

IAGO
Be wise, and get you home.

EMILIA
I will not.
IAGO offers to stab EMILIA

GRATIANO
Fie!
Your sword upon a woman?

EMILIA
O thou dull Moor! that handkerchief thou speak'st of

I found by fortune and did give my husband;
For often, with a solemn earnestness,
More than indeed belong'd to such a trifle,

He begg'd of me to steal it.

IAGO
Villanous whore!

EMILIA
She give it Cassio! no, alas! I found it,
And I did give't my husband.

IAGO
Filth, thou liest!

EMILIA
By heaven, I do not, I do not, gentlemen.
O murderous coxcomb! what should such a fool

Do with so good a woman?

OTHELLO
Are there no stones in heaven
But what serve for the thunder?--Precious villain!

He runs at IAGO IAGO, from behind, stabs EMILIA, and exit

GRATIANO
The woman falls; sure, he hath kill'd his wife.

*No, I will as openly as I want.
God and men and devils, all of them
Can say that I am shameful for speaking, but I will.*

Be smart and go home.

I will not.

*What!
You draw your sword to attack a woman?*

*You stupid Moor! That handkerchief you were talking about
Was the same one I found and gave to Iago.
He often, and very seriously,
Giving an importance to it that such a small thing does not have,
Begged me to steal it.*

Evil whore!

*You think she gave it to Cassio! No! I found it
And gave it to Iago.*

You trash, you are lying!

*By God, I am not lying, gentlemen.
You murderous, conceited man! How did such a fool
Get such a wonderful woman?*

*Why won't God throw down stones at Iago
Like the ones that make the noise of thunder?
-- You villain!*

This woman has fallen: he has killed his wife.

EMILIA
Ay, ay: O, lay me by my mistress' side.

Yes, yes, place me next to my mistress.

GRATIANO
He's gone, but his wife's kill'd.

He is gone, but his wife is dead.

MONTANO
'Tis a notorious villain. Take you this weapon,

Which I have here recover'd from the Moor:
Come, guard the door without; let him not pass,

But kill him rather. I'll after that same villain,

For 'tis a damned slave.
Exeunt MONTANO and GRATIANO

He is the worst kind of criminal. Take this weapon
Which I have taken from the Moor,
And come, guard the door outside. Do not let the Moor pass,
But kill him if he tries to leave. I will go after Iago;
He is a damn slave.

OTHELLO
I am not valiant neither,
But ever puny whipster gets my sword:
But why should honour outlive honesty?

Let it go all.

I am not very strong
If every little wimp can take my sword.
But why should my reputation go on longer than my honesty?
It's all gone.

EMILIA
What did thy song bode, lady?
Hark, canst thou hear me? I will play the swan.
And die in music.
Singing
Willow, willow, willow,--
Moor, she was chaste; she loved thee, cruel Moor;

So come my soul to bliss, as I speak true;
So speaking as I think, I die, I die.
Dies

Lady, what did your song mean?
Can you hear me? I will be like a swan
And die singing.

Willow, willow, willow–
Moor, she was pure and loved you, cruel Moor.
I swear by my soul I speak truly,
And as I speak my honest thoughts, I die.

OTHELLO
I have another weapon in this chamber;
It is a sword of Spain, the ice-brook's temper:--
O, here it is. Uncle, I must come forth.

I have another sword in this room.
It is a Spanish sword, tempered by ice water –
Here it is. Uncle, I am coming out.

GRATIANO
[Within] If thou attempt it, it will cost thee dear:
Thou hast no weapon, and perforce must suffer.

If you do, it will cost you your life.
You do not have a weapon and so you will suffer.

OTHELLO
Look in upon me then and speak with me,
Or, naked as I am, I will assault thee.
Re-enter GRATIANO

Look in at me and speak to me,
Or, weaponless, I will attack you.

GRATIANO
What is the matter?

What is it?

OTHELLO
Behold, I have a weapon;
A better never did itself sustain
Upon a soldier's thigh: I have seen the day,
That, with this little arm and this good sword,
I have made my way through more impediments
Than twenty times your stop: but, O vain boast!

Who can control his fate? 'tis not so now.
Be not afraid, though you do see me weapon'd;
Here is my journey's end, here is my butt,
And very sea-mark of my utmost sail.
Do you go back dismay'd? 'tis a lost fear;

Man but a rush against Othello's breast,
And he retires. Where should Othello go?

Now, how dost thou look now? O ill-starr'd wench!
Pale as thy smock! when we shall meet at compt,

This look of thine will hurl my soul from heaven,

And fiends will snatch at it. Cold, cold, my girl!
Even like thy chastity. O cursed slave!

Whip me, ye devils,
From the possession of this heavenly sight!
Blow me about in winds! roast me in sulphur!

Wash me in steep-down gulfs of liquid fire!
O Desdemona! Desdemona! dead!
Oh! Oh! Oh!
Enter LODOVICO. MONTANO, CASSIO carried in a chair, and Officers with IAGO, prisoner

LODOVICO
Where is this rash and most unfortunate man?

OTHELLO
That's he that was Othello: here I am.

LODOVICO
Where is that viper? bring the villain forth.

OTHELLO
I look down towards his feet; but that's a fable.

Look, I have a sword,
One better than any that laid
On a soldier's leg. I have,
With this single arm and this good sword,
Fought through more obstacles,
Twenty times more, than your guard. But what an arrogant comment!
It is not like I can control my fate.
Don't be afraid, even though I have a weapon.
This is the end of my journey,
The last place my sail will take me.
Are you backing away in fear? It is not necessary.
Rush against my chest,
And I will back down. Where should Othello go?
O, look at you, Desdemona, your cruel fate!
As pale as your nightgown! When we shall meet at the end of time,
This look of yours will throw my soul out of heaven
And demons will take it. Cold, cold, my wife!
You are as white as your purity. O I am accursed!
Devils, whip me,
And keep me from looking at this angel!
Blow on me with the winds of hell! Roast me in sulphur!
Wash me in lava fire!
O Desdemona! Desdemona! dead!
Oh, Oh, Oh!

Where is this poor, reckless man?

You are speaking of him who was Othello. I am him.

Where is that snake, Iago? Bring him forward.

I look down at your feet, but it is a fable that the devil has cloven hooves.

If that thou best a devil, I cannot kill thee.

Wounds IAGO
LODOVICO
Wrench his sword from him.

IAGO
I bleed, sir; but not kill'd.

OTHELLO
I am not sorry neither: I'ld have thee live;
For, in my sense, 'tis happiness to die.

LODOVICO
O thou Othello, thou wert once so good,
Fall'n in the practise of a damned slave,

What shall be said to thee?

OTHELLO
Why, any thing:
An honourable murderer, if you will;
For nought I did in hate, but all in honour.

LODOVICO
This wretch hath part confess'd his villany:
Did you and he consent in Cassio's death?

OTHELLO
Yes.

CASSIO
Dear general, I never gave you cause.

OTHELLO
I do believe it, and I ask your pardon.
Will you, I pray, demand that demi-devil
Why he hath thus ensnared my soul and body?

IAGO
Demand me nothing: what you know, you know:

From this time forth I never will speak word.

LODOVICO
What, not to pray?

GRATIANO
Torments will ope your lips.

If you are the devil truly, I will not be able to kill you.

Take his sword away.

I bleed, sir, but am not dead.

*I am not sorry about that. I want you to live,
Since to me, death is happiness.*

*Othello, you used to be so good,
But then you fell victim to the words of this damn slave.
What can we say about you?*

*Anything.
Call me an honorable murderer if you want.
I did nothing out of hate, but everything from a sense of honor.*

*This villain has confessed part of his plans.
Did you and him plan together for Cassio's death?*

Ay.

But general, I never have you reason to think poorly of me.

*I believe you, and I ask that you forgive me.
Will you please make this half-devil speak
And say why he tricked my soul and body?*

*Ask nothing from me. You know what you know
And I will not say anything every again.*

Not even to pray?

Torture might make you talk.

OTHELLO
Well, thou dost best.

Do whatever is best.

LODOVICO
Sir, you shall understand what hath befall'n,

Which, as I think, you know not. Here is a letter
Found in the pocket of the slain Roderigo;
And here another: the one of them imports
The death of Cassio to be undertook

By Roderigo.

*Sir, you will soon understand everything that
has happened,
Which you do not, yet. Here is a letter
That we found in Roderigo's pocket,
And here is another. One talks about the
Death of Cassio and how it was meant to be
accomplished
By Roderigo.*

OTHELLO
O villain!

That villain!

CASSIO
Most heathenish and most gross!

So ungodly and disgusting!

LODOVICO
Now here's another discontented paper,
Found in his pocket too; and this, it seems,
Roderigo meant to have sent this damned villain;

But that belike Iago in the interim
Came in and satisfied him.

*And here is another letter
From his pocket. This one, it seems,
Was from Roderigo, and he meant to give it to
Iago
But then Iago
Came in and killed him.*

OTHELLO
O the pernicious caitiff!
How came you, Cassio, by that handkerchief

That was my wife's?

*O evil scoundrel!
Cassio, how did that handkerchief come to
you
That was my wife's?*

CASSIO
I found it in my chamber:
And he himself confess'd but even now
That there he dropp'd it for a special purpose
Which wrought to his desire.

*It was in my room
And Iago just confessed
That he dropped it there for his own purposes
Which he used for his desires.*

OTHELLO
O fool! fool! fool!

Fool! fool! fool!

CASSIO
There is besides in Roderigo's letter,
How he upbraids Iago, that he made him
Brave me upon the watch; whereon it came
That I was cast: and even but now he spake,
After long seeming dead, Iago hurt him,

Iago set him on.

*In Roderigo's letter,
He criticizes Iago for making him
Anger me during the watch where I
Was assigned, and he even admitted just now,
Though he looked like he was dead, that Iago
hurt him
And tricked him to do it.*

LODOVICO
You must forsake this room, and go with us:
Your power and your command is taken off,
And Cassio rules in Cyprus. For this slave,

If there be any cunning cruelty
That can torment him much and hold him long,

It shall be his. You shall close prisoner rest,
Till that the nature of your fault be known
To the Venetian state. Come, bring him away.

OTHELLO
Soft you; a word or two before you go.
I have done the state some service, and they know't.

No more of that. I pray you, in your letters,

When you shall these unlucky deeds relate,
Speak of me as I am; nothing extenuate,

Nor set down aught in malice: then must you speak

Of one that loved not wisely but too well;

Of one not easily jealous, but being wrought

Perplex'd in the extreme; of one whose hand,
Like the base Indian, threw a pearl away
Richer than all his tribe; of one whose subdued eyes,

Albeit unused to the melting mood,
Drop tears as fast as the Arabian trees
Their medicinal gum. Set you down this;

And say besides, that in Aleppo once,
Where a malignant and a turban'd Turk
Beat a Venetian and traduced the state,

I took by the throat the circumcised dog,
And smote him, thus.
Stabs himself

LODOVICO
O bloody period!

GRATIANO
All that's spoke is marr'd.

You must leave this room and come with us.
Your rank has been removed,
And Cassio has been placed in charge of
Cyprus. As for Iago,
If there is any cunning torture
That can keep him in pain for a while but
alive just as long,
He will get it. You will stay as a prisoner
Until your crimes are known
In the Venetian government. Bring him away.

Wait, I want to say a word before going.
I have worked for the government, and they
know that.
Nothing more needs said there. I ask that in
your letters,
When you talk about these bad events,
Talk about me as I am in reality. Do not
exaggerate
And do not write about me in anger. Describe
me
As someone who did not love wisely, but did
love a lot,
And say that I was prone to jealousy, but was
manipulated
In the extreme, and say that my hand
Like a foolish Indian, threw away a pearl
Worth more than his whole tribe. Write that
my calm eyes,
Not used to being sad,
Give off tears faster than trees from Arabia
That are known to let drip their sap. Write
this,
And say also that once in Aleppo,
Where a dangerous Turk wearing a turban
Beat a Venetian man and slandered the
country,
I took the Turk by the throat
And killed him like this.

What a bloody ending!

Everything that has been said is bad.

OTHELLO
I kiss'd thee ere I kill'd thee: no way but this;

Killing myself, to die upon a kiss.
Falls on the bed, and dies

CASSIO
This did I fear, but thought he had no weapon;

For he was great of heart.

LODOVICO
[To IAGO] O Spartan dog,
More fell than anguish, hunger, or the sea!
Look on the tragic loading of this bed;
This is thy work: the object poisons sight;
Let it be hid. Gratiano, keep the house,

And seize upon the fortunes of the Moor,
For they succeed on you. To you, lord governor,
Remains the censure of this hellish villain;
The time, the place, the torture: O, enforce it!

Myself will straight aboard: and to the state

This heavy act with heavy heart relate.

Exeunt

I kissed you before I killed you. Now it is fitting
That killing myself, I die kissing you.

I was afraid of this, but I thought he did not have a weapon.
He was a passionate man.

You dog,
Crueler than sadness, hunger, and the sea!
Look at the dead bodies piled onto this bed:
This is your work. This is a poisonous sight,
Someone cover it. Gratiano, take care of the house
And take the Moor's estate,
For it all goes to you. And you, Cassio,
Must punish this criminal.
Enforce the time, the place, and the kind of torture.
I am returning to Venice immediately to tell them
In sadness the awful events that happened here

CPSIA information can be obtained
at www.ICGtesting.com
Printed in the USA
BVHW010315120521
607048BV00006B/1963

9 781629 178400